# HOW TO LOVE AN
# ADDICT

2nd Edition
Originally published 2011
"How to Love an Addict"

# HOW TO LOVE AN
# ADDICT

*Therese Small*

**BALBOA.**PRESS
A DIVISION OF HAY HOUSE

Balboa Press books may be ordered through booksellers or by contacting:

Balboa Press
A Division of Hay House
1663 Liberty Drive
Bloomington, IN 47403
www.balboapress.com
844-682-1282

www.howtoloveanaddict.life

Unattributed quotations are by Therese Small

Print information available on the last page.

ISBN: 978-1-4525-3201-1 (sc)
ISBN: 978-1-4525-3203-5 (hc)
ISBN: 978-1-4525-3202-8 (e)

Library of Congress Control Number: 2011900875

Balboa Press rev. date: 07/11/2023

# CONTENTS

# DEDICATION

This book is dedicated to my son and all those who struggle with addiction. Whether you love someone who is addicted, or if you are addicted, the trauma is the same for us all because we are all human. You aren't alone; there is hope, never lose hope.

# PROLOGUE

$\mathscr{A}$ddiction is complicated. This book is not intended to interfere with or replace programs such as Alcoholics Anonymous' 12 steps, or other programs. These programs play an important role in recovery, as do counseling, healthcare and properly prescribed medications.

Even addicts who are experiencing periods of sobriety may have cravings, whether it's gambling, sex, eating disorders, hustling or a variety of other addictions not related to drugs or alcohol. These addicts can be just as volatile. Addiction triggers can still cause the peaks and valleys of euphoric and depressive states of mind that can have an effect on behavior.

If you feel your life or general well being are in danger, please seek physical safety, legal or mental health assistance. Sometimes addictive behavior can be unpredictable and dangerous, so assess your individual situation properly.

Everyone has a story and a unique experience. We can know someone else's story if they choose to share it with us, but we can never understand someone else's experience. Our lives and opinions are shaped by our experiences, and our experiences are created by our senses; they are as unique as our thumbprint. As we create better experiences in our lives, maybe our perceptions and opinions can change. This is my story and how changing the way I respond and creating new, better experiences in my life helped me heal.

Everyone is worthy of love, and everyone is worthy of respect. We are all just a work in progress, whether we're an addict or someone who loves an addict. At the baseline of our humanity, we all want the same love, acceptance, respect and security. Sometimes when people are affected or afflicted, they just can't accept any of these things at that moment. It doesn't mean they don't want them; it just means that they've changed the chemistry of their brain and body, and they aren't in their "right" mind. Practice non-judgment and learn to look at human similarities, rather than our differences. I know how hard this can be; that's been one of my most challenging experiences. But, one thing I have learned without question is that sorrow and trauma, and happiness for that matter, are the same for us all.

The Law Enforcement Officer experiences the same trauma as the felon. The Physician experiences the same trauma as the patient's family. The person who loves an addict experiences the same trauma as the addict. Because we are all human, our emotions are the same and the process by which we heal those emotions is the same. The suggested healing principles in this book will work for everyone, but only if they apply them. It's not enough to learn about something; you have to experience it and come to know that it is true.

I would like to recognize the exposure to addiction in my life as a gift and for teaching me so many lessons about acceptance and unconditional love. I respect the suffering of the addicted as part of the process, and I've come to respect my own, as well. There is a lesson in all suffering, crisis, and conflict, if only we become conscious of it, and once we've done that, well then everything can change.

The only way to love an addict is to love yourself first. The only way an addict can recover is to love themselves first. It doesn't matter who you are, or what your story is; we are all the same when it comes to digesting our traumas and grief and starting the healing process. It's always and only about love.

The principles I share here, I have experienced for myself. They transformed my life entirely. Now I teach others and help others shift their experience toward a more fulfilling, healthier, more spiritual existence. Each of the pragmatic steps has a dual purpose for creating real transformation physiologically and spiritually. There are literally thousands of qualified studies to support the conclusions of science regarding this information, and there are Physicians who teach it and apply it in their practices. With new technology, we are beginning to see that what used to be perceived as "belief" is now being paired with science. Technology can now be used to measure things like changes in energy transference, changes in human biology when someone is thinking about or practicing their faith, changes in the brain and biology when someone is meditating, changes in energy when someone is in the final stages of death. This is so fascinating and in and of itself provides hope! Where there was room for argument in the past regarding the effect of faith, prayer, meditation, and other mindful activities, the room is getting smaller leaving less room for argument! The effects are now measurable!

If you are like me and question everything, pubmed.gov or the Integrated Studies Health Archive & Research website (ISHAR) are good places to start to find some of these studies. This is not a research project; this is my story and this is a story of healing; it is a story of my experience. These healing principles are originally of Hindu origin and according to the Vedas. My own Native American culture has similar principles in honoring the Five Elements of the Universe, the Earth and the Four Cardinal Directions. Some well known Philosophers who have studied and written about these principles include Schopenhauer, Spinoza, Haggle, Decartes and Emerson. This is only skimming the surface of the depth and beauty of these principles, and I am only including here the pragmatic, immediate, day to day practices that can help you begin the healing process and help you find your faith; whatever that is and however that works for you. This is step by step instruction for how to find your higher power.

I wish these principles were mine and that I could take credit for their development, but I cannot. I simply know they work through application and experience. These principles are timeless and will work just as well for you as they have for thousands of others for more than 6,000 years. It is my hope that you will use the wisdom herein to enrich your life first, and then the lives of others. This is a consciousness-based approach to living that provides greater well-being, a sense of peace, awareness and joy, even under the worst of circumstances.

# CHAPTER ONE:

## *My Story*

*I* have witnessed and been affected by addiction in many areas of my life and have teetered on the edge myself. I had a very charmed childhood and when I was around 8 or 9 years old my parents took in a foster child. They had a few other foster children before, and a few after, because they were just good people like that. But this particular child was only 3 weeks old and had been taken from his biological parents. The child had been found alongside the road in an automobile full of people who were passed out drunk, and also high from huffing fumes; the child was also unconscious.

This beautiful baby boy had been born prematurely, in a bath of cheap wine, and at 3 weeks of age, weighed less than 5 pounds. My father is a big man, and could hold the baby in the palm of one hand. I instantly fell in love with him; I dressed him, coddled him, fed him, and bathed him. Because of my age it didn't seem like work, it was more like I got a new doll; but this one was alive. He had a bassinet in my room next to my bed and sometimes I put him in bed with me. I remember him crying and crying for hours on end, and can remember my mom leaning over the bassinet to take him out of my room and soothe him. The poor little guy suffered from various bouts of pneumonia, allergies and colic, but also withdrawal. We didn't know too much about all of that until much later. He had been born an alcoholic with a weakened immune system and cognitive issues that wouldn't show up until he started school. Not too long after he came to stay, along came another.

The second boy was the biological brother of the first, and was just 15 months older. He had been taken from his biological parents too, before this other baby had even been born. He had been put in an extremely abusive foster home, and after the abuse was reported, then he was brought to us. The biological parents of these two brothers had a total of 6 children, all of whom would be removed from their home. Eventually, the two boys who had come to stay with us were adopted by my parents. I had one older biological brother, and now 2 younger brothers. One of them is Fetal Alcohol Effect and the other Fetal Alcohol Syndrome. Our family as a whole has had to deal with many barriers these kids faced related to the cognitive and behavioral symptoms that result from this kind of gestational abuse. Their biological mother passed away at the age of 38 due to complications from liver cirrhosis, and their biological father stopped drinking later in life and began to forge relationships with the three of his six kids who were still living, and the grandkids he now had. No one resents or judges them, because people can't be who they really are until they manage to regain their right mind. In this case, it took him several years, but at least he's tried. It has to be an excruciating task to have so many years lost to addiction and then try to patch all the holes you've managed to punch in the proverbial walls. Some of the holes can't be patched and you have to live with the loss and sorrow of that, as well. Fetal alcohol birth defects are 100% preventable, but what is done is done and the brain can't be repaired after the fact. Fortunately, the relationships can if everyone involved is willing. Even though there is a lot of heartache experienced when a child is born affected like these beautiful boys, it's the brain that is broken, not the heart.

I remember my mom sitting at the kitchen table and crying along with them when they couldn't learn something at school that seemed easy for other kids. I remember them on their hands and knees at night, rocking back and forth for hours. I remember the outbursts of anger or emotion when they experienced the inability to express their needs. What they did know, for sure, was love. It didn't take them long to learn that everyone around them loved them so much and that it was okay to return that love. Into adulthood, they both turned out to be wonderful fathers and grandfathers thanks to my parents' generosity and love. Have they both had their own struggles with alcohol? Yes, they have; they had a predisposition to the disease. Substance abuse has a substantial genetic component for Native Americans, which they are, and their genetic makeup lacks some of the protective and immune building factors, like metabolizing enzyme variants. They had immediate barriers from conception, just by being exposed to alcohol and substances in the womb, and then also by having DNA that is lacking in these protective factors.

Alcohol was also at the forefront of my marriage for many years, also. During the course of time we'd been together, we attended marriage counseling twice, spent countless hours arguing into the wee hours of the night, with no resolution of course, and jeopardized every part of our relationship. It always takes two, but when one person is primarily foggy from the effects of alcohol, it makes everything less clear. When I first met him we were young and he was a blast. He always drank more than I was comfortable with, but I thought I'd found my soulmate, and went right along for the ride. Our relationship was volatile for the first few years. It was passionate and tragic, all at the same time. As I matured physically and emotionally, I began to see the way things really were, rather than the way I wanted them to be. I tried everything I could, at the time, to make things better, or different, from my perspective. I tried drinking with him, I tried being sad, I tried being angry, I tried complacency, I tried begging, I tried talking, all to no avail. Nothing seemed to make him see things my way.

The journey was somewhat lonely, but it's been mine. It was only lonely until I really dug deep and found the path to my own solution. Such beautiful experiences can be born of so much trauma and sadness. I have learned to love unconditionally; I've learned that we are all different in some ways, yet all extremely common in most ways. I am the one who has changed. I am the one who has begun to question a deeper level of happiness, a deeper level of existence. When I decided to change myself and my own perception of things, I was at a place in my life that was the emptiest emotional state I had ever been in, yet at the same time, I felt fuller than ever; more full of joy, more full of peace, more full of contentment. I felt self-confident and capable, and able to manage myself and my life. I think it felt empty and full all at the same time, because I had decided to stop looking in the rear view mirror and start looking through the windshield. I also learned a lot about practicing detachment. It felt like a new beginning. I organized my relationships as #1 my higher power, #2 myself, and #3 all others. I found that once I latched onto that higher power and made it primary in my life, I could approach everything else in life with a sense of detachment. It wasn't that I didn't care about everything and everyone and what was going on, it was just that I started to maintain my own balance and focus on what was important to me first.

It was somewhat strange though, because at the same time, I felt like I had suffered the loss of a very dear friend. Had I outgrown this person who shared my home? When we were younger, the man I had lived with drank at home on occasion, usually just one or two, but the majority of his activity took place at local social events, and at bars, lending to the fact that he was rarely ever home. He was a social drinker and almost always the last one to leave. I think because he was gone so often, it was easier for me to stay in the marriage and to create what seemed like my independence.

I can't begin to detail the multitude of dysfunctional events that occurred because of alcohol. His drinking led to countless hours passed out in a chair until the wee hours of the morning, driving while intoxicated, nearly starting the kitchen on fire from passing out and leaving food cooking on the stove. There were birthdays that had been forgotten, feelings that had been hurt and infidelity that had occurred, saturated in a drunken stupor which just made me want to puke even thinking about it. Many, many times, I had been completely and totally embarrassed in public by his behavior, which led me to stop going out with him altogether when I knew we would be in that environment. There were many times when he was drunk, he flirted with or made lewd comments to other women in front of me, other times when he carried on with derogatory comments toward me in front of others, and whining conversations about me and how irritating I could be to him. So many times the following day, he would pretend as though nothing happened, or just simply deny that it had. Most of the time, he could not remember that it had happened at all.

For most of our time together, the extent of his alcoholism was shared by me with only my closest friends. I kept it from our families for the most part, and I became used to ignoring the situation and going on with my life. The shame of addiction carries the same weight in our lives, whether you are the addict or someone who loves the addict. Fortunately for me, I am a person who looks for positive things in my life that fulfill me, and I don't mind spending time alone. I learned to go to the movie alone, and grab some dinner alone. It can leave you pretty empty inside though, when you're trying to understand this low level love of a relationship like that. He was a functioning alcoholic, so I used to question myself and wonder if I was the one who was overreacting. The person who was independent of this excessive drinking behavior is a wonderful man at his core. He is thoughtful, sensitive, kind, hard working and extremely family oriented. This is the person I have stayed for, well that and the kids and grandkids, of course.

My first step in my own process of change was to structure my life around making sure I wasn't around him when he was drunk. Much of his time was a vicious cycle of drinking one day, and being hung-over the next; the situation was always extremely predictable.

I practiced relief through release and tossed out the fear that he would leave me if I decided to live my own life my way. I knew I would be fine on my own anyway; I just didn't want to put our kids through a divorce, I didn't want to move, I didn't want to divide up all the lifelong friends we had. I just didn't want to bust up the family! Isn't it a curious thing that we'll put ourselves through "all that" thinking something else is worse.

Every time, and I do mean, every time, something happened in my life that was traumatic for me, the death of my 4 grandparents, countless issues with my youngest son, tragic issues in his own family, and a variety of other emotional events that occur in our lives, he was at some local bar. Whenever I needed my partner to be there for me to tell me everything was okay, he was not there until decades later when we were both older. So many nights I would lay in bed and cry, not sleeping until he was home. Many nights I would go to bed and drift off to sleep, only to be awakened to the door slamming, the refrigerator door creaking, and then him crawling into bed in the middle of the night, after the bars had long since turned off their signs. I would methodically get up and move to the couch or the spare bedroom in an effort to salvage a few more hours of sleep, and to avoid the smell of him and his locomotive-like snore. His selfishness and simple inconsideration made me so angry when I'd wake in the morning exhausted, sore, and irritable.

The final beginning of the end for me was a high school class reunion. He had never attended any of his class reunions before, and made quite an entrance at this one. He came home to get ready for it, already having visited the local cantina and well on his way to an eventful evening. He made a complete fool of himself, and that night, I was not proud to stand by his side. I knew a few people there, but for the most part it was my first time meeting most of them. We mingled and I spent much of the evening performing damage control and watching him bump into the walls as he walked back and forth to and from the restroom. Two women actually approached me and asked how I was able to "put up" with his behavior. These were perfect strangers mind you, and I was completely mortified. I promised myself then and there, that would be the last time I would allow him to do that to me. Was he doing this to me or was I doing this to myself? I promised myself that even though there lived a good man inside the dysfunctional one, I would risk losing everything in my life to have the peace and joy I felt I deserved. That was my first awareness that I was truly ready for change; when I realized I would literally risk it all! I finally developed the courage and conviction to take my life back.

This marriage had been a continuous cycle of dysfunction and I allowed it to affect every moment of my life. I continued to function as well as I could on my own, but decided that being alone and lonely was far better than being with someone and being lonely. The incredible difference in this personality when drunk was staggering. I began to examine it and it became my catalyst for change.

The relationship had, at times, been extremely painful for me. I had never really been able to express that out loud, or to admit how really bad things had been. Even when we went to counseling he somehow convinced the counselor that he was a good husband. He brought me roses and random gifts sometimes and that bowled her over. After that, it was almost impossible to "convince" her of my side of the story. However, there had also been good times, too; many, many good times. It was not until the point that I made *an internal* decision to change my life, that he decided to change his. Call it fate, call it destiny, call it whatever you wish, but once my thought process and my actions, and *primarily my reactions*, changed, it was then that I noticed a change in him. Sometimes age has a lot to do with things changing, also, but addicts have a unique sense of fear of not being the center of attention. Once you make the determination to make yourself the center of attention again, and care about them from a distance, they get confused.

In changing myself and the situation around me, I was forced to not only respond differently to the addictive condition, but also to really do some soul searching and take a good long look at myself in the mirror. This was probably more painful than realizing that my reactions must change, in order that the status quo may change. It was not my fault he was an alcoholic. However, because I had taken on the entire management of our life, it allowed him the freedom to go to work each day, stop off for a drink on the way home, and have no other responsibilities. I had become the perfect enabler. I made sure everything was in order for him so that he could continue his cycle of destruction with no interruptions; with no accountability. I hid our dirty little secret from pretty much everyone except my closest friend.

Once my decision had been made to make a change, I began to push and then gently shove some of the responsibility, and accountability back on him. If things he needed to do or accomplish did not get done, I left them undone, instead of running to make sure they were taken care of. It took some self-managing control on my part, but I was finally able to accept what really was my responsibility as a healthy, functioning adult, and let him do the same. I mustered up the courage to tell him the truth about why I would not go places with him, or why I did not wish to speak to him at certain moments. He reacted with anger and I responded with confidence. I let him know that I had too much respect for myself to put myself in those positions again. That made him very uncomfortable, but as is with addiction, it gave him an excuse to drink some more.

I once read an article about marriage and alcoholism written by a Psychologist. He said that the only way someone can stay in a relationship long term if one person is an alcoholic, is if the other person is codependent. He said that both are addictions and the codependent is actually the sicker of the two people. Well, after that I felt like someone punched me in the gut! Talk about serious soul searching! I had never heard it put like that before. I knew I was codependent, but that started at an early age when I was helping to care for my two younger brothers on a pretty consistent basis. When I really dug deep and did some self-reflection, I saw how I had just been so busy in my life making sure everyone else was always okay, and that things were running smoothly, I didn't even know who I was or how I had gotten to that point. The person who had written this article also pointed out that it is imperative that the codependent person leave the relationship if the alcoholic doesn't get sober. My belief is that everyone needs to make that decision for themselves. Everyone's story and situation is unique, and everyone has a life that is like their own.. I don't think one shoe size fits everyone and that one model for health and healthy relationships works for everyone. While I do agree that relationships are very sick when addiction is involved, you can become an example in your own life, and for others around you. You can learn to contribute and make everything in your own life more meaningful. Sure, sometimes the relationship will end, but sometimes you can find a pot of gold at the end of the rainbow, too. The most important thing for me was changing the order of my relationships, making my higher power my #1, and creating a better relationship with myself for myself. Because my spouse was gone so much of the time working 12 hour shifts and then at the bar, it made it easier for me to stay in that kind of relationship, I think. He was never home and I was alone a lot (except for the whole busy working mom thing) so that allowed me to implement some of the things I was learning.

I have watched close friends and family members lose their entire "self" in the haze of drugs and alcohol abuse; some managing jobs and family, and managing to stay afloat instead of drowning in a sea of dysfunction, others participating in recovery, and others choosing simply to deny that it plays any major part in their life. But, my most traumatic and trying experience has been the meth and opiates addiction of my youngest son. His substance abuse started early in life, before he was even 13. Of course, it didn't start out with meth; it started with huffing and marijuana. Because of his addictive nature and tendencies with which he was born, his abuse and aggressive addiction didn't take long to root and involved marijuana, cocaine, heroin, prescription pills, meth, fentanyl or probably whatever he could get his hands on, but gambling too. He once told me gambling was the worst addiction he had. That revelation floored me! His drug addictions were extreme and I couldn't imagine gambling being worse. The warning signs were all there early on, but I chose to ignore them. I chose to deny that I should be the one who would have a high school dropout and become the mother of a drug addict. Our other kids had always been relatively socially "normal" (whatever normal means), and had gotten decent grades and participated in sports and other extracurricular activities. My son continues to live his life one day at a time and tries to fight the good fight, but I live my life in constant fear and constant prayer having faith that he can stay clean and manage to outlive me.

He is truly one of my dearest friends, and one of the most compassionate, intelligent and loving individuals I have yet to meet. I thank him frequently for the insight he has provided in my life. His, and my own, suffering have allowed me the lessons of non-judgment, acceptance, altruistic love, and spiritual growth, the likes of which I never thought I could experience. Sometimes I feel an enormous amount of guilt when I think of the spiritual path I've come to know, but probably never would have discovered had it not been for him. I almost feel like I've somehow gained from his painful existence. Sure, I had been forced to make some serious changes because of alcohol issues in my marriage, but one of the most painful things you can experience is watching your own child literally dying right in front of your eyes. There have been many times over the years when I thought the finality of death would be easier than just watching someone I love so much die slowly.

For the longest time, I asked myself why I was given this son with such extreme issues. Why me?! Hadn't I been a good mother, hadn't we given him everything? His addiction and all of the resulting circumstances took so much from me that I had been forced to make huge physical and mental changes in my life, or die! Literally! Eventually he was diagnosed as having Bi-polar Disorder. This explained a lot!

I had a very lengthy labor and excruciating delivery with him when he was born. When he was a baby he was rigid when I would hold him. He didn't melt into you like a newborn does. As he got a little older I would try and play patty-cake with him and he would just stare at me. I would lay him down for a nap and when I'd go to check on him, he would be sitting in his crib playing patty-cake by himself. During his toddler years and early elementary school years, he threw horrible tantrums and cried; they were out of the ordinary emotional outbursts, and the crying lasted for a long time. He had struggled in school and social activities for years, and I did not know how to help. I was forever being called by the school and meeting with teachers, and even the Principal sometimes. Most of his youth, and young adulthood I practiced damage control, just as I had done with my husband. It's difficult to admit that your child may have a mental illness, which I know now is no different than other illnesses; it needs to be treated!! Medications and therapies have come a long way in the past 20 to 30 years and continue to expand into body-mind-spirit treatments. There still is a stigma attached to mental illness, though, and most people are afraid of what they don't understand. I've learned more than I ever cared to know about it, mostly the hard way, but unfortunately at the time, I just did the best I could with what I knew. There again came more shame and denial, both on my part and his.

He was an awkward teenager and didn't fit in easily. He was bullied constantly once he got into junior high. One day when he was in the lunchroom a group of guys grabbed the sandwich he was eating and stuffed it down his throat in front of everyone. Another time two kids on the football team grabbed his backpack from behind and pulled it halfway down his arms, and then shoved him down the stairs. He wasn't able to catch himself or recover because his arms were tied up in the backpack. It was really painful physically and emotionally. It's difficult to understand the pathetic entitlement of kids like that. I really, really wanted to go to the school and just kick their ass! I did go talk to the people in the office the following day, but of course, nothing was done.

As I have grown older I've learned a lot about highly sensitive people and I've learned a lot about being empathic; in spite of his extreme addictive nature, he is both highly sensitive and empathetic. Only about 20% of the population are highly sensitive people. They process things differently than the other 80%. They have an extreme propensity to be disturbed more than others by violence, trauma and feelings. They are very much more likely to be linked to higher levels of creativity, deep emotional bonding with other people, and have a great appreciation for beauty. Their senses seem to be heightened, but living in a world of noise and confusion is so difficult for them. That kind of sensitivity can bring a lot of pain in a world where 80% don't understand. I don't think I understood enough when he was young, but I sure do now!

My husband had suffered several bouts of unemployment after working for the same company for nearly 25 years which put our finances in jeopardy. The company he worked for had gone out of business and forced everyone into a layoff. In our small rural community, jobs like his were difficult to replace and he had struggled to find another long term place to fit in. By this time, my son had been in juvenile detention 3 or 4 times for various behavioral issues and then after turning 18, in jail several times. What started out as mischief or low level misdemeanors, began to escalate. I was forced for a period of time to work 3 jobs, and also assist in running our small part time business, while trying to keep up with my son's various court dates, disappearances, middle of the night phone calls, and medical issues. Around the age of 16 he was diagnosed with bradycardia. He saw a few doctors and one of them said he was lacking hormones and had not developed properly. I took good care of myself when I was pregnant, and he was well cared for as a child. However, his drug use started during his pre-pubescent years and just continued to get worse which literally stunted certain developments of his physiology.

One of my jobs required a huge amount of travel. I was lucky enough to have been able to work from a home office with all of my work. However, working 12 and 16 hour days, traveling, trying to maintain our business venture, and juggle all of the dysfunction caused by my husband and my son, at one point, I just felt that I needed to simplify my own life so my physical and mental health could be reinstated. There were days where I literally felt like I was dying inside, and some days I just wished for it. My grandma's voice would always ring through saying "when life gives you lemons, make lemonade!" I miss her every day of my life no matter how long she's been gone! She had a story of her own and it was a rough one for a while. She had always stayed cheerful and upbeat, no matter what, even through three rounds of cancer. I vowed that I would be the same kind of example to my grandkids and make the same mark on their life. That has proven to become true. I don't think I could have accomplished that without the memory of my grandma, without having come so close to not wanting to live anymore, and without having discovered the beauty of Ayurveda in my life.

We had our 3 other children, some of whom were having families of their own now, and this one individual, this 4th child, seemed to get all of the attention; all of the negative attention. I was literally at my wits end, and suffering from exhaustion. I had made a decision to take a full time position with less than ½ the pay I was currently making, and to put our part time business as a second priority. Eventually, after 7 years of operation, the business venture just had to go. I had come to the point where I was completely spent and I didn't care if I lived or died. Even if no one else had, I had hit my rock bottom. At that point, I literally felt like I was treading water with barely enough strength to keep my head above water, and I was slowly heading for the falls!

My husband was able once again to secure work, and it opened up a window of time for me when I could finally breathe. I looked back over the past several years and could absolutely not recall how I had gotten to this point. I felt like a Salmon swimming upstream all the time. I had started to experience debilitating migraines, and experienced a 9 month long illness that no doctors could find an answer for. Doctors attributed the migraines to fluctuating hormones; my question was at what point in our life don't our hormones fluctuate!? All it did was piss me off even more! By this time, my son had been in the emergency room overdosing, and had been in and out of jail multiple times. At one point he did overdose and the friends he was with threw him in a bathtub and threw ice on him repeatedly. I didn't know this until many, many years after. I'm sure there is a lot that I will never know, and I'm also sure there is a lot I never want to know.

In his early 20's he spent 8 weeks in an inpatient treatment center but they put him on so many pills ending in zone and zine, his eyes were literally rolling around in his head. His tongue was thick and he could barely speak. There was no way he could absorb anything they were trying to teach him, and recovery? How does that happen when you trade one drug for another? About 2 years after being released from the treatment center his addiction got even more aggressive. He spiraled downward and out of control so fast it even made my head spin. Meth is the ugliest, most evil mistress! Meth is horrid and meth relapses just have such a malevolent, violent, dark horror to them, it defies description.

One day he was headed to turn himself into the county jail for some misdemeanor charge (I can't even remember which one) when he received a call from a friend. The friend asked him to go to a neighboring state with him. He and this friend had been friends since childhood and they considered each other as brothers. My son turned his car around and headed back to meet the friend; that impulsive decision proved to be one of the worst of his life. The intention of what was about to happen in the neighboring state was all bad. Both of them were arrested on drug charges and he ended up spending 4 ½ years in prison. When I first found out about everything that happened, I thought well he can sit there. This is the time when he has hit a brick wall and needed the lesson. If I had known what was about to happen, I certainly would have intervened again, because that's what codependents do, and

I would have tried to salvage even some of what would transpire. This was about the same amount of time I had migraines. I figured out for myself that they were psychosomatic and stress related, but not until years later. What was right in front of my face, I was unable to see at the time. My son is 6'2" and when he was arrested he weighed about 120lbs. He looked like a skeleton of a person.

During the time he was in prison, I began to take back my life, one day at a time, one hour at a time, one minute at a time. It felt very selfish at the time, but I knew where he was, I knew he was being fed and had access to medical care, and I was at the end of my rope. I began to practice mindfulness and learn everything I could about living a more peaceful life. I began to write and poured out my soul onto paper. Sometimes I'd write short stories, or sometimes poetry, or sometimes I would just vent onto the paper. It became my retreat and my getaway. Fairly regular journaling is still a tool I use today to "get the ugly out." It just soothes my soul somehow. I also started to learn a lot about various methods of energy healing so I could use them on myself. I just dug deeper and deeper into studies of consciousness and healing because like everyone else, I wanted to know, needed to know, why! Why was my son an addict and why did this happen? I thought I could find the answer to addiction, but the answer I found turned out to be entirely different. The answer I found was the answer to everything.

I had always told my son there were 2 places I never wanted to visit him, one was in prison, and the other was at the mortuary. I had in fact told him that if he did end up in prison, I would never visit him there. That proved not to be true. He was incarcerated for 8 months before I was able to visit, and I really couldn't wait to see him. During his time in the state system, he was moved 5 times in that 4 ½ years. It was increasingly difficult to visit him in person because eventually it was a 10 hour drive, one way, just to get where he was.

I went through the ridiculous process of lecturing him and asking him why! Of course, he had no answer; only remorse. The only good thing that came of all that drama was the fact that he was officially diagnosed as Bipolar. That itself answered a whole lot of questions about his behavior as a child and beyond. He had been diagnosed as having severe depression at the age of 13 by a Counselor and I blamed it on the drug use. I know now that he had a predisposition to addiction and later recognized the hereditary and genetic factors. There are still days I'd like to beat myself up over not seeking more intensive treatment for him when he was young, but could have, would have, should have all day long doesn't change the past. He had a paternal Uncle who had similar issues and eventually died at the age of 34; they even look alike.

His friend was released from prison before he was, and to this day I still don't know why. It was the friend's car, the friend's drugs and the friend's agenda, that landed them both in the system at that level; but it was his split second decision to participate that catapulted him into the equation. My son's friend wrote me a letter while he was in prison and apologized for taking my son with him and provided me with some of the details. While I tried to resent him for a while, I couldn't. My son was a grown man at this point and had made the choice to do what he did. The two of them had been friends since they were kids. The friend had a terrible childhood with no stability and at one point had even lived in a car with his mother. My son had a very different seemingly middle-class childhood, but addiction has no respect for social boundaries nor class. The friend returned home from the nearby State after his release. He started using again shortly after, went to a party, overdosed, and a carload of people dropped him on the sidewalk in front of the emergency room of the local hospital, naked and wrapped in a towel. He died there on the sidewalk, alone and naked, 6 weeks after his release from prison. I did not want to tell my son about this in writing; I wanted to be there for him. On the next in person visit with my son, I had the gruesome responsibility of telling him that his friend he considered to be a brother was gone. He didn't take it well. We sat there at the table in that sterile prison environment with other people all around us, and prison guards looking on. I reached across the table and grabbed his hand, but only for a moment until a guard came and said please don't touch the prisoner. I was unable to even give him a hug. He shut his eyes so tight I thought they'd never open again and he choked on his sobs. He knew he couldn't and wouldn't let himself cry; it wasn't allowed there and it was in fact, dangerous to let your guard down and show any kind of emotion. So many emotions have been stuffed so deeply inside of him for so many years, my heart bleeds for him. This on top of the trauma he experienced while in the prison system, led to an additional diagnosis of PTSD after he was released.

After he got out of prison and had been sober for 4 ½ years, he would go on to start using again within 6 months of his release. He would have extended stays in three different hospital psych wards over a period of 4 years and more jail time. At one point,

$20,000 was paid to a private rehab center to try and get him more treatment. He left the program after 7 days and the money was non-refundable. After a few more years he was put into a mental health treatment court, and went through another 90 day treatment program, which this time he completed. He had a girlfriend who had been incarcerated and she had been released while he was in treatment. After he finished the treatment program he went to see her. She said some really unkind things, probably defensively because she had to focus on herself now. He was very hurt and got drunk with a friend. He was still bound by the court to drug test and tested positive for alcohol. Because it was so soon after the 90 day treatment the judge kicked him out of the mental health court and reimposed his original sentence. He rarely, if ever, drank alcohol. It certainly wasn't his drug of choice, but this was his addictive brain telling him that now that he had finished treatment he was in control of his addiction and as long as he wasn't using drugs, he was okay. "It's okay, just go ahead and drink; it's not like you're getting high, you'll be fine." It's the numbing they are looking for; the ability to feel nothing is so much less painful than having to feel the shame and deeply buried emotions, but is it?

So much paperwork, so many lawyers, so many counselors, doctors and psychiatrists, so much documentation is stored it could be used as a foundation to build a house! It seemed it was always the money stopping me from putting him in a long term, dual diagnosis treatment, but later I had spent thousands and thousands of dollars on legal issues and other things. The 90 day treatment he completed was a dual diagnosis program, but how do you untwist decades of dysfunction along with mental illness in 90 days? Is that even possible? Does this kind of story ever end?

Probably only in the death of one party or the other; or the death of the relationship as it is. That may sound harsh, but isn't it the truth? The trauma has to be dispelled somehow, either through change or death, but the past is ever looming even if the addict is able to stay clean. It's difficult to let go of or repair decades of destruction.

An addict just wants to be an addict because it's just too scary to change. They must have a reason to get clean; they must have a purpose or a motivation that is important enough to them to stop. You cannot, and will not, determine what that reason is. At one point what I thought was rock bottom for my son came after I changed the way I was living and changed my responses to his requests and behavior. He stated to me that "he just didn't care anymore, and that he was just going to go all out." He basically was on the highway to hell, and didn't care at that point whether he lived or died. One of his counselors relayed to me that in one court appearance he told the judge "my mom is giving up on me." Of course I wasn't giving up on him, I was just putting myself first now and not reacting to his drama. I think this made him afraid and vulnerable, and for the first time, he could see that I was going to try and be okay no matter what. They call that radical acceptance in treatment. I practiced it myself and had radically accepted that no matter what happened or how this whole thing ended, I was going to be at peace, one way or another.

He was extremely negative and derogatory during the first part of his prison incarceration. As time passed, and his body began to sober up and heal, his remorse and regret became much more evident. He stated at this point, that he was done, and that he wanted to change his life. I had heard those words many times before, but what seemed to be different this time was that he expressed a need to give back.

He expressed a need to approach a drug court of which he had been a part of, and had never finished, and express to them his gratitude for their help. He also expressed a need to write to judges and other members of the court and express his forgiveness and gratefulness. These were things I had not heard him speak of before. He began to change during the same time in which I began to change. I had had enough of the violation of my personal space, and he had had enough of the dysfunction and hurting the people he loved. When I decided to dig a moat, he decided to extend a hand and help me dig that moat.

I will never "let down my guard," so to speak, simply because once an addict always an addict. Still within him dwells the battle of good vs. evil, as it does within us all, but tends to be a little more dramatic in the confines of addiction. But to have him express so much love, so much remorse, and so much talk about prayer and how it was beginning to change his life, literally, made my heart swell. He was actually becoming "aware" of the change in his life, not just talking about it. This change or shift of awareness happened within the confines of a state prison. Unfortunately, his obsession took over once again, but at least I had gotten a glimpse again of that person I loved so much. Once a person experiences that hope, that desire for change, and learns a few things they can use as tools for change, they always have that to hang onto, even if they relapse. It's almost like a rope with knots; you have to use the knots to climb the rope and sometimes you slide back down, but you reach up and grab another knot and get to the top one step at a time. I have no intention of painting a rosy picture of what it might be like in a prison cell. This was not a summer camp he was sent to, but he was trying, and he spoke of hope for the first time in a very long time.

It gave me hope to think that he could manage to make a few simple changes, and maybe even experience a little bit of healing while incarcerated. Imagine what you can do to change your awareness and thought process while you are free!

Even in recovery there is a certain sadness that comes. During his stay in prison, my son and I were only able to communicate via written correspondence. I tried to communicate with him at least once weekly. In one letter I included a newspaper clipping in which a former addict had written a letter to the editor expressing his remorse and regret for the troubles he had caused in his community. I found the letter very inspiring and uplifting. I cut the letter out of the paper and mailed it to my son as a point of inspiration.

As he had begun a second round of recovery, he was bitter about the fact that I sent him the article, and perceived it as me reminding him of his past, rather than trying to encourage him by pointing out someone else's victory. Negativity and blame are not only great friends of addiction, but they are also pretty close acquaintances of recovering addicts. I was reminded by my son that when I sent him news of the happenings in his family, and information regarding drug abuse, it "stressed him out," and he didn't feel that he needed the additional stress in his life right now. It made me angry because he hadn't given me or other members of his family any regard during the many years he caused us undue stress. We didn't ask for that. We cared deeply about him and spent many years walking on eggshells in an effort to try and help him "heal." I did not get the privilege of asking him not to cause any undue stress in my life, because I had other children to attend to, a husband, a full time job, a small business and extended family situations in which I was involved. I sure wish he would have asked because my answer would have most definitely been a huge NO!, and please don't cause me any stress I can't handle right now.

That had been my initial response, but then I learned to start to have respect not only for my own changing experiences, but his too. I had no idea what was happening in the confines of that prison, but I began to try to understand what he was going through. Simultaneously, he was going through withdrawal, experiencing grief, experiencing the vulgar, rough environment, but then also experiencing a renewed faith, hope and love. I knew this was nothing I would ever be able to comprehend, and I grew to have an enormous amount of empathy for him. The lessons I learned during this period of time were first to change how I responded to his anger, and second that it doesn't matter who you are or what your circumstances are, we all have the same emotions. Sure, we have a unique story, but feeling sad or feeling bad or feeling anger is the same for everyone. That led me to my next realization that if everyone hurts the same, then everyone has to heal the same. I realized, and respected the fact, that my son was a felon in a prison and that I was a mom unable to get to my child, and we both felt the same. We were both experiencing trauma and heartbreak on the same level, but for very different reasons.

During one of his periods of incarceration in a county jail, a woman called me to tell me that she had a son incarcerated with my son. They had been arrested and I had been unable to visit my son for a variety of reasons (one of the reasons being that I had finally begun to realize that rushing to his rescue one more unsuccessful time was serving no purpose to either of us.) I had finally realized that it was necessary for him to skin his knees a few times more in order to figure out how to stop falling off the swing! That was really immature thinking on my part, but I didn't know that until later, either.

She had visited with my son while visiting her son. The two men had become friends, and my son asked her to contact me and let me know he was okay, and find out if I was okay. Up to that point, my son and I had been communicating through written letters only. This woman, who I did not know, and who I had never met, called me. She proceeded to tell me how her son was a good kid, but had gotten in with the wrong crowd. She said that they had started drinking and had started to burglarize homes. Her son was 18 at the time. I seriously doubted that he had just started drinking and that his drinking led to burglarizing homes. That behavior is more indicative of someone looking for income to get their next fix. I simply stated to her that my son had a very serious, long standing drug abuse problem. She said that her son did not use drugs and didn't have that big of a problem, but reiterated that he had gotten in with the wrong crowd.

In my heart I felt such sorrow for her denial; I had been there. Here her son was 18 years old and in jail for burglary, and she was pretending that he had gotten kicked out of class. In my mind, I thought to myself, well lady, my son "is the wrong crowd."

*Pretending that things are not as bad as they seem serves no purpose. At the first signs, it's bad and can only get worse.*

When my son was in high school, I received a call from the school my son attended. They called to let me know that he had been caught huffing air spray used to clean computer keyboards. All I could think or say at the time was, "kids do the darndest things." His side of the story was that he and another boy in his class were "messing" with one of the girls in class. She had gotten angry with them and told the teacher they were huffing from the can. I could not believe that my son would actually do something of the sort and let the school officials know. Had I known then, what I know now, that would have been the beginning of the end of my enablement. I was always afraid to get the police involved because I did not want my son going through life with a long police record. Because I did not seek to get him the correct help, but instead sought to deflect every time he was in trouble, it ended up costing me literally thousands of dollars, and felony charges and prison time for him. He got a long police record anyway!

I'm a mom, so there have been plenty of times that I have blamed myself for his prison time, for his addiction and for every other wrong thing in his life. Is it my fault? Maybe part of it, maybe I could have rescued him early on if I had been more mindful and aware then, but I wasn't. I've beat myself up over and over wondering about all of those things. All of us have things we carry into adulthood from our childhood, so one thing I have learned is that at some point he needed to start the process of taking responsibility for his own actions. I can be blamed for allowing his behavior to continue on. My extreme codependency and lack of respect for myself and my own boundaries helped him carry on. Everyone has their own rock bottom, but you can't know what that may be until it happens. You will see the most appalling things happen, and think that the shame and the embarrassment, and the physical ailments will certainly be rock bottom, only to find out that the dysfunction continues. And it escalates! It seems like after a period of sobriety and then a relapse, the behavior gets more aggressive; it is this unstoppable monster that is unimaginable. You don't want everyone to know that your life is in constant chaos or that there is this level of dysfunction in your life! You see, the person who is diseased with addiction and the person who loves this addict experience the same trauma, the same emotional and mental suffering, the same shame and embarrassment! It is the same because we are the same. We are spiritual and human at the same time, and our needs are the same.

One of the times my son spent time at the psych ward at a local hospital, I thought that was my rock bottom. I certainly thought that it may be his as well. He was placed on psychotropic drugs that turned him into somewhat of a zombie (again!). I knew that he was still in there somewhere, but was unable to even reach out to him at this point, because now, he felt nothing at all. His mania with meth had been so extreme, and in an effort to allow his body to try and begin to repair the damage he had done, they were trying to fix his drug issues, with more drugs. I felt like someone had kicked me in the stomach so hard that I may never breathe again. Eventually he would add opiates and opioids to the mix to self-medicate. His very sick brain tricked him into thinking he could control his addiction and control his ups and downs and dope sickness.

Rock bottom for an addict must be a turning point in their own reality. You can't know what that is, so don't waste your time trying to figure it out. They will know when the time comes for them, but it's important to understand that time may never come. Not every addiction story has a happy ending, unfortunately. My own son, during one eight week stint in rehab, was simply not ready to participate. He was adamant that he did not have a problem, and that he did not need counseling. He did not participate to the fullest extent, but only waited to get sprung, so he could start all over again.

*The simple reality of it all is that their rock bottom may be death, and sometimes addicts are already dead inside, but they cannot die.*

During the various times he was locked up, I would write to him and I would weep. I would weep in my car, I would weep in my sleep, I would weep in the bathtub and I would weep after I hung up from talking to him on the phone. I had become a master enabler to everyone in my life and I wondered, did that make me as sick as everyone else? I believe yes, it did. I knew I needed to learn how to heal myself first. All of the decisions that followed and the emotions that came along with them, have allowed me the courage to share the lessons I've learned, and to hopefully, help even one other person change their life for the better.

Not long after my son's release from prison, he and a friend just happened to stop by our house. They were in my son's car and had parked it by a shop located behind our house. They came into the house, really nonchalantly, and asked if I could give them a ride to the friend's house. I asked my son why he hadn't just dropped his friend at home before he had come to our house. He stated that he had no gas and that they had come from the other direction, a nearby town about 20 miles north of ours. I said sure I'd give them a ride. We loaded into the car and backed out of the driveway. As soon as I had backed out of our driveway into the public street, I was immediately surrounded by 4 vehicles. I was confused and surprised and an officer jumped from one of the vehicles in full protective gear, with a gun drawn. He opened my car door and ordered me out of the car. I can't begin to describe the shock and state of confusion I was in. By the time I exited my car, I was surrounded by 8 armed county sheriff's and U.S. Marshall's; each of them had a gun pointed directly at my head. I live in a very quiet, rural area, and this was just something you don't see everyday. Some of the officers opened the back door of my car and removed my two "passengers." They placed them in the prone position on the ground and one officer escorted me up the driveway to my house. I was crying and shaking uncontrollably and trying to find out what was going on. The friend of my son had a felony warrant. An officer had attempted to pull them over on a county road and they had eluded the officer and parked the car at my house. The officers took the two young men away, and I was allowed to pull my car back into the driveway and fall into a weak, weeping pile of hysteria. I could not, and still today, have a hard time believing that happened. My son had no warrant at the time (which was highly unusual), but was taken in for questioning, and the other "friend," was arrested. That was one of those experiences that leaves an imprint on your person so deep, you can vividly remember it years later like it was yesterday. Near death experiences have a similar effect; I know because I had one when I was about 3 years old. I thought that I should never forgive my son for that incident. There had been many incidents before, and many after that as well, but not that extreme. I could have been shot and killed right in front of my house because of someone else's decisions and lifestyle. I was driving a Prius and living my life on the right side of the law for God's sake, and I didn't even have a speeding ticket on my record! I was a compliance executive working for a government entity. This was not supposed to be a part of my life. I was terrified and horrified! That was a pinnacle turning point in my relationship with my son. In the end, I forgave him, but I will never, not ever, allow myself to be put in a grave situation such as that ever again. I decided to use that terrifying experience as a lesson and another point of change.

My story was first published in 2011; I was foolish enough to think my story was over. Four years before this rewrite began, my son was arrested for eluding. He was pursued while he was driving, and in his impulsive way he pulled over, jumped out of his car and ran. By the time that happened there were 6 officers who had joined in and he was chased on foot. He threw a bottle of water at an officer and then was caught, taken to the ground and beaten by the six. He was taken to the local hospital and received stitches and care. His glasses of course were broken and he was battered and bruised, but not terminally. He was charged with eluding and sentenced to two years in prison. Three years later, he had not been put in the prison, but had been moved around the system into and out of programming. He was then committed to a mental health court. One year later, a total of four years after he had been arrested, he had failed to meet all the requirements of the mental health court and he was then sent to prison for the second time, for his second felony. One judge commented on record that he would be given credit for all time served (which had already exceeded his original sentence), and one judge (the final judge) commented on record that he did not do that. He had been sentenced to two years, and it had already been four in and out of the county jail. No matter what happens, he will have ended up serving at least double the amount of time he was sentenced to. Collectively, since he was 14 years old, he's served more time than most people who have committed heinous acts; all for being a drug addict and having a mental illness. I'm sure it's been at least 10 years and it seems like it is all for nothing. We have an extremely broken justice system where Public Defenders are underpaid and overworked. The only goal is to get a plea accomplished and get the file off their desk. Unfortunately, there is a person in that file, and that person has loved ones who are also affected. Sometimes we get exactly what we deserve, and sometimes there is no justice. Prisons and jails are a festering ground for addiction and mental illness, but a necessary evil to keep society safe. Society doesn't need to be saved from my son, my son needs to be saved from himself.

One thing I know for certain is that karma is an accumulation of our life experiences and the results of our decisions. It's been a lifetime since this story began, and I don't know how it will end, except for the death of one or the other of us. The meaningfulness of finding your higher power and living a life of giving rather than collecting, a life of service rather than selfing, a life of humility rather than arrogance, is all we need to know. I still feel sad, angry, disappointed, depressed sometimes, but I process those feelings and let them go. I feel happy, joyful, peaceful and content, too, and I choose to hang onto those feelings and not let them go. I have a steadfast faith in what works for me now, and for that I am truly grateful.

I grieve my son every single day of my life. I cling to the lessons I have learned in connecting with the Earth, energy healing, and experiencing an altruistic higher love in my life. Without these things I fear I would not be able to make it through. The practices keep me grounded and they keep me going for the other people in my life. Grief can be all consuming and can literally drive you to an early grave. I refuse to allow that. My grief is my own and I can either choose to hang onto it not knowing what will happen in the future, or I can choose to live in each second, each minute and each hour of the day in a way that heals me, and that promotes healing for everyone and everything else. I need people to know they are not alone. Losing someone you love is hard and there is a grieving process for that, but grieving for someone who is living is a pain and suffering without relief. It has to be managed and it has to be digested, and then it has to be replaced with the opposite of grief. It's the only way. The extreme and profound experiences I have during meditation have helped me not to fear death, for anyone, and to understand that living with purpose is the only way to live; to truly live and feel alive.

*Suffering is not a necessary part of proving love! You can love someone who is living or someone who has passed without attaching yourself to the suffering. It is possible. It is possible to choose to be happy even under the worst circumstances.*

I am not an expert on addiction, but I am experienced in dealing with addiction, and what I have become, is an expert in managing my response to addiction. I am an expert at making sure that my cup is more than half full, and an expert at believing that I have made mistakes and forgiven myself for them. I am an expert at making sure I have forgiven others who have wronged me. I am an expert at working toward a higher, richer, better life and I have become my own caretaker, and my own biggest fan.

I still suffer from being a member of the human race, but I think I finally get it. You cannot get drawn into the multitude of little dramas that occur each day; you have to just create a certain level of peace in your tiny little space, and peace of mind, and judge only yourself by your response to situations. Risk not reacting to every situation, to save yourself; risk responding differently than you ever have, to save yourself; *risk losing everything* to live a life that is right, a life that is rich and full. Come to know that sometimes doing nothing at all is the best response. When you are at peace, the answer will come naturally, so choose response over reaction, every single time.; choose peace.

Having and maintaining a better quality of life, only enhances everyone and everything around us. Small miracles occur in a smile, a kind word, or just a gesture of charity; when we make someone else feel better we automatically feel better. It is okay to be boring instead of engaged in chaos. It is okay to get out of the house and take a walk to take in all that nature has to offer instead of repeating yesterday's behaviors. It is okay to express your joy when everyone around you is in tears. It is okay to feel good. It is okay to wish for all the riches life has to offer. It is okay to forgive yourself and others. It is okay to leave yesterday in the dust and head for a brand new dawn. It is okay to say no. It is okay to turn your back on all the drama and even turn your back on the past. It is okay, because you are okay.

*I was once told that if everyone threw their troubles into a bucket, you would probably reach in and pull yours back. Somebody always has it worse!*

My hope is that by sharing what I have learned about healing and moving forward, you might be assisted in your journey. I hope you are able to find even one piece of advice within the pages of this book that may help you to be happier. Life is never perfect, and we shouldn't expect it to be. However, when such incredible suffering is in our midst, we can still make the choice to be happy moment by moment.

I know, from personal experience, how difficult and complicated this can be when your heart is breaking wide open and your grief is so strong that you feel like you might die. I know how difficult it is to keep your mind on the most simple of tasks, when all you can think about is that the person you care about might not live another minute. I know what it feels like not to know where they are, but you know for sure they are continuing to destroy themselves. In order to move through the tragedy of the situation, you must make a first move. Otherwise, you will be stuck living in this tragic melodrama until the end.

If you think things are bad at the current state, when you begin to change yourself, you must prepare yourself for the worst. The addict in your life will not take lightly to the fact that you have decided to stop your enablement, and to reach out and grasp the life you want. They will not take lightly to the fact that you have chosen not to make your life all about theirs. Take care of yourself first and prove to yourself that you have the strength and determination to get what you deserve.

Sometimes we have false hope and just wait for everything to be perfect before we make a move. That is never going to happen. It takes one tough individual to live with, and love an addict, so don't ever think you aren't tough enough to get out if that's what you desire. Our home should be a safe and sacred place. We don't want to upset the apple cart, so we stay, and make sure that what appears on the outside isn't exactly what is going on, on the inside. Very often, the nicer the front door, the bigger the secrets hiding behind the door. Open your front door; leave the screen door open, flying in the wind. Show your real face and don't pretend to be someone you're not. Don't make the mistake of pretending that problems don't exist in your home; you are only as sick as your secrets. Don't be ashamed to have suffered dysfunction in your life, and don't wear the shame that addiction brings to us all. Experience a higher level of being and understanding; no one is above you and no one is beneath you, and everyone no matter who they are has issues in their life. Learn and develop the strength to deal with your issues on a very different level, and then help others with theirs. Make a real home. A home where you know you can be safe. A home where you can be yourself, and a home where you can live the life you deserve to have.

When you can survive solely on your instincts and intuition, and when you can find happiness without seeking outside yourself, and when you can be alone, and still feel peace without feeling lonely, and you can feel happiness and joy in the midst of chaos, then you are truly home.

Make each decision in your life purposefully by learning the principles of grounding and mindfulness. Strengthen your inner core and your courage. Strengthen your opinion of yourself and your worthiness, and mostly, strengthen your faith. Seek the answers from a force much greater than you can ever imagine. It will guide you, and it will sustain the very life within. This can be accomplished through religious practices, through meditation, through spiritual discovery, through a variety of ways that connect us with the earth, with all other human beings, and with the scientific laws of the universe. The only way for the light to get in is through a crack; sometimes hearts must be broken in order that the light can come in and start the healing process. This requires faith.

# CHAPTER TWO:

## *Don't ask why*

*I* could write an entire book about my son's life, but it isn't my story to tell. I used to think it was; I used to think I knew how he felt and what he was thinking, but that's never true. Even if someone tells you what they think and how they feel, there's no way to encapsulate the thousands and thousands of thoughts we have a day into a summary of what we think. Our thoughts and our emotions are fleeting and ever changing. We might be able to express what we think and are feeling in the moment, but half an hour from now it may change. He writes poetry that I've read, and I've read his journals from treatment and from prison. Still, he was only capable of expressing what he was feeling in the moment, and what he had experienced in the past. As I read, I formed my own opinion, based on my own experiences, which would differ largely from his.

I only know what I have experienced, I can't possibly know what someone else's experience has been. No two people can have the same experience in this life; it is impossible. Even siblings who are raised in the same home by the same set of parents have vividly different experiences because they are a result of our perception. Every individual has their own perception of the world, and forms their own opinions and reality through their personal experience. Just like DNA, they are uniquely ours.

Addiction is the subject of much study and scientific research, and it's complicated! It's very difficult to pinpoint what causes it and why, because again, everyone's experience is different. Long term use can cause the body systems to become used to something, and then this "thing" the person is using or doing becomes their norm, or more of an obsession. They need to do or use the thing they are obsessing over in order to feel normal. Some people may only try something once and be hooked from the very first time. Sometimes these obsessions bring on violence and malevolence; sometimes they bring discontent and indifference. Eventually, in pretty much all cases, reclusive behavior can occur because of shame, embarrassment and self-loathing; these are all common feelings of someone who is addicted. In the throes of this obsession some will lock themselves away to indulge, some will form the inability to keep a job or function at the most basic level, or some may be the person who masks their addiction in the midst of what appears to be normal social activity.

I am a chronic dog rescuer. I always have 2 or 3 at any given time and have had up to 5 at one time. My son told me once seeing an animal suffer is the one thing his poor heart can't take. I think of all the things he's done and probably seen in his lifetime, and he still has the tenderness to really love animals. He has brought more than a couple into our home, which I of course end up caring for while he's a ward of the system. I really don't mind though; probably part of my codependent nature. They are the best company! I walk them every day all year long, rain or shine. It takes a lot for us to miss our walk. I already mentioned I live in a rural area, so not a lot of traffic or activity. On my daily walks, I noticed a few years ago that someone who lives not too far from me is an alcoholic. There is a road behind our house that leads to a subdivision with homes that are upscale in price. Everyday, in the same place along the road, there are mini bottles of liquor, or cardboard single serving containers of wine, or cans of flavored malt liquor. When I first started noticing them I was so irritated that someone would be throwing their trash out the window like that. Then it didn't take long for me to start to notice a pattern. These things are disposed of in the same places on a routine basis. Someone who is hiding their alcoholism at home is getting off work and ritually drinking before they get home. It's pretty clear after all these years that they don't care what type of alcohol it is, but the pattern of where and when they drink it is hurried and obvious. It looks like they have been able to time themselves in order to get a certain amount of alcohol ingested between work and home, and the containers are always tossed out in the same spots. It's really sad and sometimes while I'm walking along and listening to the birds sing, I wonder about their home life in the evening and if they've experienced all that I have.

There are some risk factors that enhance the possibility of addiction including genetics, emotional disorders, environment, and abuse, but they are not concrete predictors. Certain drugs also have more addictive tendencies, and users may become addicted simply due to the physiological changes that occur with the use of the substance, and the psychological damage and effects that follow. With some, eventually your body just can't live without them.

With all these physiological changes comes the changes in behavior we cannot tolerate. This is the most noticeable symptom of addiction. Someone you thought you knew so well just changes into this horrifically different person that you can't and sometimes don't even want to know. So, how can you possibly love an addict? Why do you stay in this situation? Why don't you just leave? How can you possibly maintain a relationship with this person? Maybe the addict is your child, or your sister, brother, mother or father, someone you can't just leave. Maybe you can't leave, but you can make a choice not to be around this person any longer, or possibly ask for help from someone you trust. Certainly if the addict is your spouse or significant other, you can make the choice to leave, or the choice to stay. There are so many different situations and circumstances, and each person has a story and each story is different. You can't attempt to decide for someone, or to judge someone for staying or leaving. You can only decide what's best for you. What causes you to leave, and what encourages you to stay is not the point. The point is to not focus on the addiction, but to focus on yourself to make sure you become the person you want to be and deserve to be.

*The only way to love an addict is to love yourself first. Remember, we all feel the same and we all heal the same. Start with you.*

You could literally drive yourself crazy trying to figure out what caused the addiction of your loved one. People have an innate need to find the cause and place the blame. Sometimes the answer cannot be found; sometimes there is no one to blame, and the cause cannot be found. So many of us just want to know why; even the addict wants to know why. I wish the "why" of addiction could be figured out. I wish it mostly for the family and loved ones of addicts. It would give us some sort of closure, some sort of explanation for the craziness our lives have suffered. Unfortunately, you will not find the "why" in this writing because I don't know why. I don't know why I've lost cousins at 30 years old, I don't know why one recovers from heroin and another just can't. I don't know why I have a son who just can't stop even though I've seen him holding his head in his hands and sobbing because he wants to stop so bad. I don't know why people minimize their addiction or minimize why they stay in a relationship with an addict. I don't know why. Good luck finding the answer anywhere outside yourself.

The most important thing you can do is understand the behavior of the addict in your life, and move forward with your own. They have a disease, and they have a disease that may not be able to be cured. The only way is to manage the disease and this is a particularly difficult one to manage. They are no different than someone with diabetes or any other disease that requires medication and therapeutic efforts, but the manifestation of addiction is different. It is the self-medication that kills them, and the behavior that kills everything else in their life. For me, the only place I've been able to find the answer is by looking within myself; no one outside of me has the answer.

Don't waste your time asking the addict why, either. It's exhausting for you and for them and they don't have the capacity to answer and they may not even know why. Often the use or activity begins as a way to numb physical pain or emotional suffering; it becomes a way to deal with trauma. Eventually, however, the physiology of the person changes and the stress, shame, remorse, regret and physical withdrawal symptoms act as fuel to keep the addiction going. Once it latches on it becomes a security blanket. If it's time to party and celebrate, they use. If they feel sad and lonely, they use. If they are in physical pain or experiencing mental suffering, they use. It becomes the justification for everything and the only coping mechanism they know.

# CHAPTER THREE:

## *Change the relationship*

*E*veryone has probably encountered addiction in some form or another. If we have not been directly touched by it, we usually know someone who has. We are all affected by the legal issues and the public chaos it creates. Oftentimes, addicts are incarcerated, or sent through rehab with public funds which affects each of us as taxpayers, even if it is not personal to us. Addiction has no boundaries; it does not hesitate to cross social classes, ethnicities, race, gender or age groups. Addiction can weave its way through business meetings, church gatherings, classroom sessions, sports activities, low income housing projects or high end exclusive housing communities. There are no limits, there are no rules, and there are no typical descriptions of an addict. It comes in all forms, all shapes and all sizes.

One commonality is that addicts tend to be extremely self-centered. This comes from their survival instinct. In their mind, they must get high again to survive. After the first time an addict gets high, which is their greatest high, they are just trying to regain that feeling again, but it never happens. They are in a never ending chase for the feeling of the first high. It's all they think about, it's all they plan for, it's all they wish and long for. Their high is the greatest tragic romance of their life!

As they chase the next high, they mow over lovers, family members, friends, employers, and anything or anyone that gets in their way. Lovers of addicts tend to be just as self centered, but without noticing, unless and until, they can gain control of themselves. When I had the realization that I was as sick as an addict, and probably even sicker, as a codependent, it knocked my socks off! When you're trying to pressure an addict, lecture an addict, persuade an addict or change their way of thinking, on any type of long term basis, it becomes more of a message of "There is something wrong with you and if I help you, it will make me feel better," or "If you'll stop, my life will be better." This is total self-absorption on both sides of the conversation. After a lengthy addiction, the subject matter becomes less about helping the addict and their health and well being, and more about making the person who cares about the addict happier. It becomes a tug-of-war of emotions, and who has the right to the most happiness, or who has experienced the most sorrow. There is a certain amount of selfishness on your part when you are playing tug-of-war with an addict. You start to play the role of a victim, and you are attempting to protect yourself and attempting to make them behave the way you would like them to behave. If you work this hard at actually becoming the person you want to be, independent of the addict, you may experience sadness and some melancholy but you will be happier on some level. Your selfishness is exhibited by continuously trying to make them better; better from your perspective. All the addict hears is that something is wrong with them. They already know this and it only reinforces their negative self-esteem and self-loathing, and then guess what they want to do? Yes, that's right, use again and some more, and some more, and some more.

By dealing with addiction in a more responsive way to create your own boundaries, you can prevent the damage that it will do to your own psyche and emotional state. Do not drag yourself into the mind of the addict; they want you there, and they will manage to keep you there, if you let them. They want everyone around them to be in as much pain as they feel; it justifies their addiction. They want to unconsciously pull you into their dramas and have you support their justifications.

Addicts will tell you many things, particularly when they are in a recovery or pause mode. They will most likely exhibit remorse and may verbalize high hopes for the future. You will know the addict is truly remorseful, and truly has high hopes for the future, when they stop sensationalizing situations, and simply commit to do better, one day at a time. They talk less about their sorrow and their future plans, and start to take action in order to move forward. Their behavior will change, but very often it's almost a sense of detachment you'll get from them. All the family will want is for reunion and reconciliation. The family wants everything to go back to the way it used to be before all the trauma. But alas, there is so much rebuilding for the addict in recovery to do if they are able to stop, it becomes their primary focus. Relapse is always looming and sometimes it's the people they love the most in their life, whom they need to detach from in order to stay the course. This isn't something you should take personally. This is them living the only way they know how in order to survive, and you need to focus on you; not them. You can't live someone else's life for them, particularly in this situation when you haven't experienced the venom and horror they have.

For an addict, there is a certain sadness that comes with sobriety; it is though they have lost their best friend. If they choose to accept treatment and begin to heal, support them in knowing that sobriety isn't quitting, it's a beginning to living. You must live by this same rule, in order not to be pulled into the ever spinning whirlpool of their addiction. Sometimes they trade one addiction for another and then the cycle starts all over again.

*Quit supporting their addiction, and begin to support your own wellbeing.*

Native American traditional healing encourages those in recovery to speak to their inner mind. They are asked to let the mind know that they have lived under the umbrella of addiction for a long time, and it has made them sick, and that now they would like to move on and try something different. They teach the acknowledgement of the power of the addiction in their lives, and teach addicts to respect the power it has, not to fear it or to plunge against it like beating their head on a brick wall. They teach the addict to acknowledge the power, verbalize the respect they have for the power, thank the addiction and the previous lifestyle for all of the lessons it has taught them, and then to gently move away from it, verbalizing that "I need to try something else for now." "I need to find something that works better at healing me and my family and loved ones."

This slow intentional movement away from negative power creates mindfulness. The power of this kind of thinking can make so many positive changes in our life if we can apply it. We can make the choice to be joyful everyday. Just as an addict in recovery must make the choice one day at a time to stay away from whatever negative power is in their lives, you too must make the choice to be happy and stay away from the negativity, one day at a time. It's okay to feel the feelings of sadness and disappointment over the addiction, but you don't get drawn into it. We have to learn to do something for ourselves *that creates the feeling of feeling good.* Internalize your happiness and the rest of the world will share it; it will shine through your eyes and your heart. I've heard it said that if you share your pain it cuts it in half, and if you share your joy it doubles! I love that. The sun is only one shining star, but the rays of the sun shine on everyone and everything alike, and they affect everything they shine upon.

Sometimes it becomes necessary to see things from the big picture view, and understand that not only has the addict become very ill, but by interacting with them on their level, we are also making ourselves ill. No problem can ever be solved on the same level it was created on, it has to be solved from a higher level. Sometimes it's cooperation, collaboration or compromise, and sometimes someone just has to shift or adjust. No one has to lose and no one has to win, but something has to change in order for the shift to happen. Enablement can kill someone; *you can literally enable someone to death, even yourself.* Chronic stress created by all of the volatile situations we experience because of addiction, is a festering ground for disease. Chronic stress can cause inflammation which has been found by the medical community to lead to a variety of health issues. Every time you feel guilty and slip them another $20, or buy them more alcohol, or let them back into your home because you're afraid they'll freeze to death, you are one step closer to allowing them to continue their behavior and one step closer to forfeiting your own well being. You are not doing them any favors and you are not keeping them safe by expressing your grief. You are only enforcing in their mind the guilt, the shame, the embarrassment, and the unworthiness that addiction brings. All of these negative emotions and feelings give them justification to continue using whatever they are using. Don't underestimate their ability to take care of themselves; they are very resourceful. This is exhibited daily in the way they manage to feed their addiction, regardless of the barriers they may face.

Their justification skills are magnificent. You yell and scream; they have an excuse to run away and get their fix. You cry and fall into a weeping pile of tears; they are ashamed and run away to get their fix. You express your love and your concern for their well being; they are embarrassed that they cannot be the person you want them to be, they run away and get their fix.

In the continuous cycle of alcoholism, there is always a reason to drink. Any reason will do; good, bad or indifferent, any reason is an excuse. Alcohol is particularly dangerous because it's legal. The excuse could be because "I've worked hard all week and it's Friday night, I deserve a break." Or, "My relative or friend died, I need to get drunk to feel better." Another one is the celebratory function, "I got a huge pat on the back today at work. You don't appreciate me, but my friends at the bar do." One person in my life used this justification: you should always have as much fun in your life as you can, while you're still able. That person used to say are you going to walk in and lie down when you die or are you going to slide in sideways (meaning into the 6 foot hole in the ground). Their idea of fun was drinking as much as possible, passing out and feeling completely terrible the following day. An alcoholic's idea of fun is always alcohol. They don't care how it affects their family or friends, or how it affects anyone but them. They don't consider that their idea of fun is really affecting, and ruining, the lives of those around them, and those that love them. At the moment, it is always about the party or the pity party. Afterward, addicts are shameful and remorseful, mostly internally, but rarely outwardly; any outward expression of remorse would be admitting that something is wrong. They can come up with any number of excuses like, we're broke, or our relationship just isn't what it used to be, or I don't feel good, or I feel really good! I'm going to get drunk. It doesn't matter, there's always an excuse and it's always the pity or the party, period!

It is the same with all addicts, regardless of the vehicle of their addiction. Though all the stories and circumstances are different and unique, the disease is the same for everyone. Their justification is always based on their emotions. Their brain says, live it up! You deserve it. You're right, you're worthless, you should be ashamed of yourself, you've hurt everyone you love, you should go out and get messed up!!! Feeling nothing at all fixes everything for them, temporarily, until they need to do it again. One of the saddest cases of all is when someone starts to experience withdrawal symptoms and they feel physically sick; dope sick is a common reference to this. They are so afraid to get sick, they have to use, no matter what! I find it so sad that they do not have the ability to see that they are already sick, and so sick they aren't willing to go through a few hours (maybe a few days) of physical pain and illness to get to the other side. They would rather use again to relieve the symptoms and stay sick with addiction; it's truly one of life's tragedies.

What a fantastic personal advisor the addictive brain can be. It will give you all the reasons why you should continue on with your destructive behavior, without you even asking it why. When we talk about the power of the mind, this is the same mind that can change that destructive behavior, and invite all kinds of positive things into our lives. We all know someone who we look at and think, why do they do that, or how can they continue living that way? And yet, we do the same. We can always justify our reasons for staying with an addict, or for clinging to an addict, or for obsessing over their addiction and trying to change them; the same way the addict obsesses over their own addiction. It is a sick, destructive cycle that only you can break. When someone is under the influence of substance abuse or other addictive activities, they do not have the power of mind or awareness to be the one to change. They simply don't have the ability to break the cycle until someone else starts the process, or until they have bottomed out and decided to seek help to change. Most addicts are powerless over their ability to do it on their own, and they are usually powerless to maintain sobriety without help. Meetings, medication, therapy and support are critical to their ability to have any shot at a "normal" life.

When you do not serve to their every whim, when you do not fall into an emotional pile of goo, they will begin to wonder why you don't care about them anymore, why you have lost your concern for them, why you don't support them in their quest for the ultimate dramatic role. This may be the pinnacle point in which they begin to change because you're not riding shotgun with them anymore.

During the worst time in my marriage, and when my son really began to speed out of control, I began to drink too much. I also gained 35 pounds. Food and wine made me feel better (so I thought.) All of the problems in my life I attributed to drugs and alcohol and here I was drinking myself to sleep, and eating myself into 4 sizes bigger. This lasted for several months and I woke up one day, looked in the mirror and thought what the hell are you doing? How are you any different? I began to justify my own behavior exactly the same way they were. Self-medication became my thing and I felt and looked terrible! Once I experienced this realization, I was terrified! How had I managed to not see what was happening? It seems like darkness creeps in slowly. Once the light has faded, it becomes hard to see anything at all. If I'm honest, I still face issues with food. I am an emotional eater, and some days I have the mindset of "I'll start again tomorrow," or "I'll start over again Monday." It's the repeat, repeat, repeat conversation that never ends. Even though I know what is right, I still have my own weaknesses and have to work to get myself back in check.

This is how insidious and destructive this behavior is, how it can continue on like a computer virus without you being consciously aware until it is too late. It is beyond the realm of ridiculous how we attempt to dull our emotions and bury our heads in the sand. Do we really blame the people around us, swimming in this sea of dysfunction, for not making us happy, for not making our lives happier and not making sure we are fulfilled? Is that a task we should take upon ourselves, or should we lay around and blame everyone around us for our unhappiness and our inability to act with emotional and mental maturity? We already know we can't trust the addict, so why do we think we can rely on them for creating stability for us? There is no one more immature than an addict. The maturity level stops for everyone around the first time they use, or when they are becoming an addicted person. It's like they are a child looking for support (every kind of support!) and sympathy. If they are one of the lucky ones and can transfigure from addiction to sobriety, they can see this immaturity in their past, but it's impossible to see when they are in the throes of their addiction.

In the study of Psychology, the nature vs. nurture debate is a long and complicated one, and is all about which one is more important. Our environment, or nurturing, certainly plays an extremely important role in our lives, but addiction can be a result of our nature, as well as our nurturing. If at some time in our life we lacked nurturing we develop issues of abandonment or feelings of not being worthy, for example. Scientific studies show that our environment also plays a huge role in relapse. Many people can overcome their addictions by focusing on a higher power. Those who hold some sort of belief system or faith, have the greatest rate of success. There must be a purpose for obtaining sobriety and maintaining sobriety; you have to have something to live for or some type of motivation to move forward. Studies have shown that by simply showing images of drugs and paraphernalia to an addict, or by returning the addict to the environment in which the drugs were used, triggers are set off in the brain similar to those that are enhanced when the addict is actually using. The triggers can set off a relapse and increase the intensity of cravings causing the person to "fall off the wagon." The act of remaining sober is more difficult than one would think, hence the adage once an addict, always an addict. The recovering addict lives a moment to moment existence in danger of relapsing.

Changing our environment can change everything for us and for addicts. Developing a relationship with a higher power or rediscovering a relationship with a higher power, requires a change in both our environment and our self-nurturing and is the best place to start. There are many qualified studies substantiating the power of faith in people's lives. It doesn't seem to matter if you have faith in a religious entity, or in a source of creation, or in science. If you are a believer in God, you have faith in things that lead you in that direction. If you have a faith in a higher being, then seek that being and bring it into your life as a position of power. If you are agnostic or atheist, you might have faith in developments in science; bring that science, the studies and the statistics into your life as information that holds power. If you have faith in the source of energy and information, you have faith in your senses that provide these experiences for you. Even if we are the person who must see it to believe it, then we have faith in our own eyes and our other four senses that form our perception of this world. You can even have faith in qualified medical studies that support the information in this book as a method of healing, and a method of changing your perception.

We all have faith in something outside of us. No matter what it is for you, never stop moving in that direction, and never stop learning. It is our duty as human beings to evolve and grow.

Developing a relationship or rediscovering a relationship with ourselves requires the same type of faith. A word of caution regarding faith, in the religious context: If your faith causes you additional suffering or guilt, find a different path that best fulfills your needs and supports your spiritual growth. It is okay to question, expand and grow toward belief systems that you are comfortable with; any belief system is better than no belief system at all (scientific studies have proven this.) Layers of guilt and additional suffering are not necessary burdens to be carried on your path to a better life. Statistics are very solid regarding recovery and quality of life, when one has a belief in a higher power. Individuals who hold fast to some sort of higher power have a much higher success rate, have better health, and seek a higher quality of living, so find what works for you, and let them find what works best for them.

You are never alone in your struggle, and you are never alone in your shame. I've heard it said that pain is physical and suffering is mental. When our physical body is in pain we can take a pill or some type of remedy to alleviate the pain. When our mind and our mental state is in pain, this is suffering. In order to alleviate that suffering we need something outside the self to reach for and to cling to; this is the remedy for suffering. This is our higher power, our source of faith. If we do not have faith in something, we then try to mask or numb the suffering with something physical or tangible. That then turns into physical pain and the cycle is difficult to break.

Also, nature and nurture are equally important when creating positive change in our lives. We can't necessarily change our essential nature or the way we were "hardwired" at birth, but we can learn how to achieve balance when our nature is out of balance, by practicing self-nurturing.

*Self-nurturing along with balancing our essential nature is the key to happiness, healthiness and equanimity in our life.*

Nature relates to genetic issues associated with predisposition to addiction, and the way we are "hardwired" when we are born. Nature also relates to the way we handle an issue. For example, if you are raised in an alcoholic home where both parents frequently drank, fought, and exhibited unsavory behavior, yet as an adult you were able to rise above that lifestyle, and chose to live alcohol free, your nature superseded your nurturing. In this case, you chose to respond to your upbringing by creating your own, different kind of life, rather than reacting to your upbringing and clinging to the dysfunction, and likely repeating your parents' behavior.

By choosing to respond to an addict, rather than reacting to the addiction, you are changing the familiar environment of the addict. Get it? You are changing the environment they are used to, and the environment you are used to. This creates real change.

*"No man gives to himself, but himself, and no man takes away from himself, but himself. The 'Game of Success' is a game of solitaire, as you change, all conditions will change." (Author Unknown)*

Hopefully, you begin to understand why trying to reason with them, or love them better is not the key to the healing of the situation. Many addicts will trade one addiction for another.

For example, an alcoholic may quit drinking and turn their consumption obsession to food, resulting in large amounts of weight gain. Addicts with money seem to require a special type of attention. They can pop pills and drink martinis for lunch, but seem to maintain a seemingly normal life during the day. To the unaware mind, they appear to have everything. However, they are no different than the alcoholic or heroin addict who is passed out on a street bench. Monetary gain or success has nothing to do with being addicted and in fact, these addicts can be the most excessive because they can afford to feed their beast.

Abusing drugs and alcohol, and over indulging in almost anything alters our brain chemistry, our moods, and our general overall well being. When an addiction is active, there are typically two states of mind the addict experiences, being high or in a state of euphoria from their fix, or being in withdrawal and experiencing all of the corresponding states such as agitation, anger, illness and general discontent. When you are trying to love someone better, or trying to talk someone into getting clean, or trying to reason with someone when they are in either of these states of mind, it is nearly impossible. You are literally dealing with someone who is not in their right mind. This is worth repeating; there are only 2 states of mind in which an addict occupies while their addiction is active, under the influence or seeking the influence.

Whether an addict is born with addictive tendencies or whether they have developed over time due to long term abuse, they are responsible for the management of their own addiction. It is their cross to bear. You cannot manage the addiction, or the abolishment of the addiction for them. Yes their life is hard because of it, and yes their life will continue to be hard because of it. Each of us has some burden we must bear, this is theirs. For them, it is a matter of life or death.

*If you make the choice to make changes right now, the next time conflict arises, you won't have to wonder how to make things different. Learning to deal with, live with, or really love an addict requires change in you.*

Our natural state of existence is bliss. The physiological function of life is bliss; our biology is bliss, but living is hard! We spend an enormous amount of effort in our lives trying to attain our external idea of bliss, only to find out the education or material items we've acquired, or the people we've attracted, or the place where we live, or the work we've achieved or a multitude of other things haven't satisfied that yearning for happiness. It is extremely common to hear about celebrities, famous musicians and well to do magnates who have overdosed and died, or exhibited some strange unacceptable behavior, or entered rehab. They chased their dreams and succeeded in getting everything they desired. So often when they are interviewed or they tell their story, they equate success with money, fame and fortune. True success is when you finally understand that you can't separate your body, mind and spirit, because they operate holistically. The stories become so cliche and the results are always the same, with just a different set of circumstances. In chasing their dreams and filling their cup, they forgot to feed their spirit. They forgot to honor and respect the source that connects us all. It isn't until they come crashing down that they realize and start seeking a deeper meaning to life. So many are so jaded by their own performance, unfortunately, their death is probably the quickest route to a deeper understanding.

Having grown up on and around a Native American reservation, I understand the power of laughter and choosing happiness, with very little in the way of material wealth. When you are grounded in your belief system and locked into your relationship with your higher power, you come to understand that the flow of material wealth is important, not just accumulating it. Gaining it, having it and then using it for helping others is key to keeping the flow going and to being content. New cars are nice, but the new wears off pretty fast. The new never wears off when you build something new or support something that goes on to perpetually help others. You do this by building a relationship with your higher power, then yourself, then all others, and staying away from all forms of self-abuse, and by not pretending to be someone who you aren't. Stay authentic! We need money to survive. There is nothing wrong with having a lot of it or having a little of it, as long as you respect the power of it and handle it in the right way. Money can become an addiction, too. If you have a lot of money and you fund charities and give a lot away, then thank you. However, if you are just throwing money at a cause and you aren't engaging with the source of humankind, the giving isn't holistic or genuine, and there is still an empty void that needs to be filled.

There are 4 keys to discovering happiness:

- You must have a sincere desire to change internally.
- You must put yourself in contact with principles that work.
- You must be brutally honest with yourself.
- You must be persistent in your quest.

When you begin to act, you will then be able to judge your situation by the actual results. You will be proving to yourself that you can do it, and you can make a positive change in your own life. Results don't lie. Even if your actions don't make a difference at first, they will eventually; science says so. Keep at it and give it your best shot, in the moment, with awareness. This creates mindfulness and raises our level of consciousness so we can make better decisions in any environment or any set of circumstances.

You are in charge of being brutally honest with yourself, being persistent in your quest, and having a deep desire for change. However, I am going to help you with the principles that work. These life changing steps are actions you can take right now to put into effect the change you need. If you truly have a desire to change, then it isn't enough to just read about it and gain the knowledge. Knowledge is something we learn; knowing is something we develop through experiencing it. Very often we have to pay for knowledge; but knowing is almost always free and comes with a shift in our experience. If our experience is a good one it can often come with grace; if it is bad we tend to suffer mentally and spiritually. Grace is a lot like the rain; it falls on everyone. Some accept it, some stand under an umbrella and some go inside and refuse to go out until it's over. The only way to create an experience of change in our lives is to apply it and see if it works for us. We do this through an attitude of faith and surrender.

I have a Master's degree and I paid heartily for that knowledge. It required no faith nor surrender, and came with no grace. I merely read things and participated in activities and I learned. It added more "stuff" to my brain that I could use as a tool, but it did nothing to change my life internally or spiritually. To acquire spiritual or internal knowing, which can't be bought or sold, we have to experience it.

# CHAPTER FOUR:

## *Step One: Understanding Who We Are*

*B*efore healing can begin we have to make a choice and we have to make a change. Remember, we have to choose to be brutally honest and we have to choose to be persistent in our quest for change. Also, because we are unique, we need to understand what our essential nature is at birth. Your essential nature can't be changed, but it can be out of balance. We are born with a certain body type and a certain set of characteristics. As a child we are innocent and we are in tune with our essential nature. However, as we grow older, traumas, grief, challenging experiences and other life events can tend to push or pull our essential nature one way or another. It kind of knocks everything off kilter and when we are out of balance, we can feel it. Intuitively our biology knows and tries to correct or overcome whatever it is that is out of whack. Addiction is an extreme example of an imbalance. People can abuse their bodies for years and somehow our amazing biology continues to try and overcome it. It is a natural process that is always working in the background trying to get us back to homeostasis, or our true nature. The same intelligence that flows through nature, flows through our biology, and we are not separate from the world around us; we are part of it.

Sometimes when an individual has a traumatic childhood they spend a lot of their life out of balance and don't have the ability to remember a time when they felt really good. Others may only remember feeling good, or in balance, as a child because of traumatic events they experience as adults. Although people and their circumstances are unique, there are certain characteristics that are common among us. When we understand these characteristics, we can understand how to gently recover our essential nature and create a better experience for living.

There are, at the most basic level, two types of stress we experience. One is acute stress and one is chronic stress. Acute stress is when something unexpected or out of our control happens, such as a car accident, as an example. Chronic stress is more of a day to day, consistent type of stress. This type of stress is often caused by us and the environment we create for ourselves. It can also be caused by environmental issues that are out of our control such as toxins in our air, food or water. Technology seems to be a huge stressor for people in our current society. It was intended to make our lives easier but has almost become the degradation of our planet and our human race. We worry repeatedly about things or expose ourselves to situations that cause chronic stress. When we are stressed, hormones like cortisol and adrenaline, for example, are created in our body. On a long term basis exposure to these stress hormones can cause internal damage and can also cause disease to manifest. The medical community is discovering that routine stress is largely responsible for inflammation. Inflammation is being found to be an epidemic, and is responsible for many auto-immune disorders and other diseases. In order to achieve our optimum level of health, we need to learn how to counteract or reverse this damage that stress can cause to our system.

As a general rule, in order to fix something you have to contradict it or apply an opposite. As an example, if you have a sunburn you don't want to put something hot on it, you want to put something cool and soothing on it to stop the burning pain. Another example could be soothing a stomach ulcer. You wouldn't want to eat hot peppers if you have an ulcer flare up, you would want something cooling that coats your stomach to stop the pain. If you are cold you put on a sweater; if you are hot you remove the sweater.

These simple examples can help us to understand how opposites balance one another, and how like can increase like. We don't put on a sweater and a coat in the middle of the summer months when it's 100 degrees outside, or we only get hotter!

The root of the science of these principles that I'm sharing with you is that there are five elements in the universe. The characteristics of these elements make up everything in the universe; even people. These elements are space, air, fire, water and earth. Sometimes space and ether are used interchangeably. In fact, ether is more correct because space indicates that there is an empty area, whereas ether is explained as a substance that permeates all space. For purposes of these concepts, we will refer to space because space represents potential. Air represents movement. Fire represents transformation. Water represents cohesiveness. Earth represents form and structure. These elements in Native America are equally important and similar in characteristics. Each is tied to a color and one of the Four Cardinal Directions which are important to our existence and learning here, and the Earth and Sky are additional and important to our creation and our sustenance.

There are three primary combinations of these five elements that determine a person's essential nature; the combinations are named and are known as doshas, these are Vata, Pitta and Kapha. The words used to describe these traits are from the Sanskrit language. Like most indigenous languages it is a beautiful, vibrational language and refers to certain meanings that cannot be translated word for word. It is important for us to understand the characteristics of our dosha because it is the blueprint for how we maintain our balance and experience better health and quality of life.

Once we know what our dosha is, then we can understand how to balance it using some very basic concepts. This understanding will assist us in first putting these principles into practice, which changes our biology, which changes our physiology, which begins the body's healing process, which then gently brings us back into balance, which then allows us to heal mentally, which then allows us to grow spiritually, which then allows us to connect to a higher power.

As we go through these doshas you will begin to recognize yourself in them and then you will begin to recognize people you know. It really is fascinating.

The first dosha is known as Vata. This dosha is a combination of space/ether and air. The governing principle of Vata is movement; you can imagine space and air creating wind. The characteristics of Vata are:

light, airy, quick, cold, irregular, mobile, changeable

As a general rule, people who are a combination of space and air (Vata) are thin framed, experience drier skin, speak very quickly, have racing thoughts, move quickly, are very talkative, usually have cold hands and feet, have variable sleep patterns, have variable digestive patterns.

When these Vata people are in balance and feeling their best, they are very creative, upbeat, have a lot of initiative but sometimes have trouble following through due to their quick thinking. They are very energetic and adaptable, and very lively in conversation. They welcome new experiences and are often the life of the party. Their habits, intentions and desires, and interests change from week to week. They are able to move from one thing to the next and bring with them a great amount of creativity and interesting ideas. They are spontaneous and can be very "forgive and forget" type people, and they can be empathic and very sensitive. They are like hummingbirds who move from flower to flower and their wings are beating some 80 beats per second!

When these Vata individuals are out of balance, the movement stops. Their natural state, or essential nature, is all about being light and airy and quick in movement, so when their essential nature is compromised (or out of balance), their spirituous traits are tampered down or increased. Being out of balance doesn't have to be one way; it can be too much or too little of one or more characteristics.

Signs that a Vata is out of balance are constipation, gas or bloating, inability to sleep, worry, anxiety, restlessness; anything that stops movement or increases movement to unacceptable levels in the body, mind and spirit. Vata people are very resistant to routines because they love change. These people are so quick and light in structure that they often forget to eat even if they are in balance, and they tend to graze and eat light snacks rather than sitting for a full meal.

The second dosha is known as Pitta. This dosha is a combination of fire and water. The governing principle of Pitta is transformation; you can imagine fire and water, with fire transforming everything it comes into contact with, and fire and water together making steam! The characteristics of Pitta are:

courageous, intelligent, focused,
precise, direct, intense, warm

As a general rule, people who are a combination of fire and water (Pitta) are medium framed, with a bit of a muscular build or naturally athletic, experience warm body temperature, speak very directly, make great leaders and visionaries, are very focused and intense, are very direct in their speech, usually have very good digestion, sleep very soundly for short periods of time, and are very discriminating and delve into the underlying issues of everything. Sometimes Pitta people even have reddish colored hair and a reddish hue to their skin color; they are all about the fire!

When these Pitta people are in balance and feeling their best, they are very compassionate, joyful, and energetic. They are very direct in their speech and don't mince words. They can accomplish anything they set their minds to. They have a very strong digestive system and are the people who have an "iron gut" and can eat about anything. They tend to have a very hearty appetite. They have piercing, intense eyes and look you directly in the eye when they are speaking to you. They run hot as you can imagine with fire and water, so they prefer cooler environments and thrive in environments where they can lead and learn. They are like honey bees, always working, moving and building and are strong in every way, but don't make them mad or you might get stung!

When these Pitta individuals are out of balance, the transformation manifests in a lot of heat! Their natural state, or essential nature, is all about being focused and driven, so when their essential nature is compromised (or out of balance), their flame begins to rise and the water begins to boil.

Signs that a Pitta is out of balance are ulcers, skin rashes, anger, intolerance, criticality, heartburn, indigestion, inflammation, irritability and harsh judgment. Pitta people are very prone to taking on too much because they think they can handle it all, and then they have too much on their plate and the stress turns into unacceptable levels of heat in the body, mind and spirit. The fire of Pitta is very much associated with sight and often Pitta's have to see to believe (or prove it to themselves).

The third dosha is known as Kapha. This dosha is a combination of earth and water. The governing principle of Kapha is structure and protection; you can imagine earth and water creating mud, clay, rocks, and solid foundations. The characteristics of Kapha are:

Sturdy, steady, consistent, heavy,
cool, moist, strong, stable

As a general rule, people who are a combination of earth and water (Kapha) are large framed and sturdy, have soft skin, speak very slowly, have deliberate thoughts, move slowly and gracefully, usually have cool hands and feet, and sleep very deeply for long periods.

When these Kapha people are in balance and feeling their best, they are very loyal, super supportive, kind, easy going, very routine oriented, and process oriented. They often have thick shiny hair, moist youthful skin, pleasant eyes and demeanor, and are consistent. They are usually very strong and naturally heavy set structurally, and sometimes have an extra layer of fat that is normal for them. They have great stamina and can go all day due to their slow and deliberate movement. These people are very loving and very easy to be around for pretty much everyone. They are like elephants who are kind and nurturing, heavy and protective, and are attached to their loved ones for life.

When these Kapha individuals are out of balance, their natural structural traits are compromised. Their natural state, or essential nature, is all about being loyal, loving and protective, so when their essential nature is compromised (or out of balance), their slow deliberate nature and their natural heaviness increases.

Signs that a Kapha is out of balance are slow reactions and a lack of motivation to change, extra heaviness both physically, mentally and spiritually, and laziness. They can become possessive and sulky, and suffer from depression, the inability to let go and stubbornness. These people are very prone to weight gain because they are structurally sound naturally. Sometimes when they are out of balance they can have the tendency to overeat and retain fluids, suffer from diabetes, allergies or congestion, and they can become needy and lethargic. The combination of earth and water compares to mucus, thickness and density when a Kapha is out of balance.

Most people are primarily a combination of two of these doshas. A small number of people are what is known as tri-doshic and have almost equal parts of all three. Everyone has characteristics of each because our body subsystems are all about movement, transformation and structure. The combinations are as follows:

+ Vata-Pitta
+ Vata-Kapha
+ Pitta-Vata
+ Pitta-Kapha
+ Kapha-Vata
+ Kapha-Pitta

Which combination you are personally depends on percentages. For example, if you have a 70% Vata, a 20% Pitta and a 10% Kapha, you would be considered a Vata-Pitta because your two highest percentages show the majority of those two doshas. There are quizzes that are taken to determine your dosha.

The first quiz determines your Prakruti. This is your essential nature at birth. These are the characteristics you are born with; this essential nature cannot be changed. In taking this quiz, you answer the questions according to a time when you felt your very best and felt the most like you. You answer these questions according to a time when you were in balance and intuitively knew it based on how good you felt.

The second quiz determines your Vikruti. These are the scores that show which doshas are governing your mind and emotions, and body at the time you take the quiz. This one shows us the variance compared to our 1st quiz (Prakruti) and it tells us where we are out of balance. You answer these questions according to how you feel at the time you are taking the quiz; how you feel right now, today.

Keep in mind there are no wrong answers. This is for you personally, and to help guide you in your healing. The only right answers are the ones that most closely align you to your dosha.

# CHAPTER FIVE:

## *Step Two: Creating a Routine*

*N*ative American philosophy views everything in the universe as a life with a purpose; nothing is viewed as separate. This includes animals, including birds and water life, rocks, plant life, the sky and beyond. The purpose does not stop with what we cannot see. It goes beyond that into the center of the Earth and above into the unknown. We are only able to actually see about 4-5% of the universe. That means there is a whole lot going on in us, around us, above us and below us that we can't experience with our five senses. We experience this with our internal, more intuitive senses. In fact, many indigenous cultures across the globe have used the planets, the stars, the seasons, the sun and the moon for keeping track of time and significant events. Our biology is attuned to the natural rhythms of the universe and nature. Each cell in our body functions in unison with these rhythms and flows between times of dynamic activity and periods of calm. When we look at ourselves independently of nature and universal influences, we immediately create an imbalance; we cannot separate our body, mind and spirit, so when we isolate one or two and only focus on one, we also create an imbalance.

There are certain rhythms that govern how our biology functions. In modern society many people ignore these rhythms altogether and customize their daily routines to fit the life they've created. It seems a little laughable that we think we have the ability to create our own being independent of the magnificence of the universe. By raging against the machine for the simple purpose of convenience, we are out of touch with the internal signals of our body and this results in poor health, extreme fatigue and accumulation of toxicity in our body. Eventually all of that catches up with us.

I read an article that reported on a study finding a direct correlation between Bi-polar people and the full moon, and movement of the planets. It really shed some light on some of the questions I had about my son and his Bi-polar disorder. The study stated that Bi-polar people were pretty much unable to sleep at all when there was a full moon. That made perfect sense to me!

Adopting a regular daily routine can be a critical step to beginning the healing process. It creates mindfulness in our activity, it lessens the number of decisions we need to make on any given day, we create synchronicity with our environment, and it puts us in a state of flow with the rhythms of nature and our hormonal system. Addiction triggers can be reduced by creating a routine that includes healthy, alternative practices to distract from the addictive, obsessive thinking. Paying attention to the rhythms of nature can take creation of daily routines even one step further by allowing our biology to work naturally and not struggle against our decisions. Very often when someone is addicted their personal hygiene suffers. The obsession they are dealing with just doesn't allow them to focus on those routine activities and sometimes they have just passed the point of caring. Their crushed self-esteem and self-loathing can get in the way of any kind of self-nurturing, even the most simple tasks.

- Celestial rhythms are the rhythms of the planetary movement
- Lunar and Tidal rhythms are the monthly cycle of the Moon around the Earth and the gravitational influence of the Moon on the Water
- Seasonal rhythms have been organized into a 12 month cycle of the Earth around the Sun
- Circadian rhythms have been organized into a 24 hours cycle of day and night

Each of these rhythms silently rise and fall with assurance, but as people we barely notice until the sun is shining on us or we're preparing for bed and we suddenly notice it's dark outside. Animal and plant life never question these rhythms. The various cycles, hours and seasons determine for them when they mate, what they eat, where they travel to, when they bloom and when they die.

When we go to bed, when we get up, what time we eat, when we work, all affect our mood and our general abilities, but we don't question it and we tend to ignore all of the internal signals we receive. Just as people have certain characteristics and a dosha, Vata, Pitta or Kapha, so does everything else in the universe. The five elements of Space, Air, Fire, Water and Earth represent the principles of intelligence that underlie all creation. Even the cycles of the day and the seasons of the year have a dosha.

Daily cycles:

+ 6am-10am - Kapha qualities, waking up slow, expelling mucus and toxins
+ 10am-2pm - Pitta qualities, Sun is highest in the sky, our digestive system is at its fiery peak
+ 2pm-6pm - Vata qualities, there's a lot of movement and creativity (believe it or not this is the best time of day to take a test!)
+ 6pm-10pm - Kapha qualities, slowing down, getting ready for bed
+ 10pm-2am - Pitta qualities, REM sleep, biological transformation is happening
+ 2am-6am - Vata qualities, body starts to stir, feeling a little lighter, biology is starting to wake up (often if you have to get up and pee after 2am you can't go back to sleep)

Based on our biology and the attunement with the cycles and rhythms outlined, there are certain activities that we can do at certain times to optimize our health. These principles are not an all or nothing, non-flexible set of instructions. We have to retain a certain amount of flexibility with our lives in order to function. The information below offers best practices for creating a daily routine, based on what is best for your biology. The less you make your body struggle to survive, the better you will feel. These are things you can start to do immediately that will help you to get grounded and start living in the flow instead of intentionally acting against it.

If you can only do two things to start with, I strongly recommend creating your daily routine and using it to reinforce good sleep. When life is in chaos and you're wrought with worry and anxiety, sleep is always compromised. We can't function normally or at any kind of healthy level without sleep. I've seen my son go days if not weeks with no sleep from the effects of methamphetamines. I can only describe the behavior and the look on his face as haggard and on the brink of insanity. Our bodies are the food we eat (sad, but true), and in addition to air, food and water, our life literally depends on the expulsion of toxins from our system and the restoration of our biology. Sleeping is one way to deal with stress to allow our body to restore, rejuvenate and renew. If we lose that restorative function, the toxins get stored somewhere else for later. The manifestation of that storage is never good.

We absolutely have the opportunity to heal by taking better care of our body, mind and spirit. If we start with daily practices of caring for our physical body it leads to an overall sense of well being, and then we become stronger mentally. Then we can change our experience of faith and if you are a believer in the spirit or the soul, that will grow organically. If you are a believer in the science of healing, well that's even easier because there are literally thousands of qualified, scientific studies supporting this information.

Our body is constantly trying to help us with our healing process and homeostasis. But if we continue the same behavior and don't make the right changes, we just get more of the same.

- ◆ Skin loses collagen but renews every 2-4 weeks
- ◆ Skeleton renews every 10 years (but slows with age)
- ◆ Every 4 min kidneys receive the total volume of body's blood for filtration
- ◆ Kidneys process approximately 200 quarts of blood every 24 hrs
- ◆ 3 quarts of lymphatic fluid filters through every 24 hrs
- ◆ Red blood cells revive approx every 120 days
- ◆ over 2 million new red blood cells are created every second
- ◆ Largest elimination organ is our skin
- ◆ Stomach lining regenerates every 5-7 days
- ◆ Liver cells life span is 150 days (cirrhosis is scar tissue, so permanent)
- ◆ Taste buds renew every 10 days to 2 weeks

If that doesn't WOW you, probably nothing will!

The morning list below seems exhausting but it literally only takes about 15 minutes or less for caring for your body, and it creates a space for you to nurture yourself before you are bothered by everyone else. If you can fit in the 20-30 minutes of exercise and 30 minutes of meditation, then you're at about an hour and a half. This shouldn't be another point of stress in your day, it should be time you spend solely on you, caring for yourself. If you need to get up 30 minutes earlier then start working on that, your health will be better for it. Once you get into these routines you will sleep better and adjusting your times won't feel burdensome. Also, regarding oils on your skin, in your mouth and in your nasal passages, only use food grade oils. You can buy these almost anywhere these days and can use a drop of essential oil, too, to create smell or sensations.

Almond oil, coconut oil, olive oil or sesame oil are readily available in most stores and on the internet (we will talk more about oils in a following chapter).

Following a daily routine creates mindfulness in our life as we concentrate on one task at a time. The purpose of the task we are focused on is to care for our body and to nurture ourselves. Just by simply performing these tasks, our biology begins to respond in a positive manner. As we begin to feel better, we sleep better, we think better and we begin to respond better. Each of these intricate, individual steps are designed to begin the process of restoration that leads to the process of healing. As we begin to heal physically we feel better, then we can focus on healing mentally. When we feel good and think good, then we can focus on healing spiritually and bring the body, mind and spirit back into balance and harmony.

Daily routines (for optimum health; do the best you can):

- Wake up no later than 6am (or around the time of sunrise)
- Try to get to a point where you no longer need an alarm and fix your room so the natural morning light comes in
- Give yourself 5 or 10 minutes to lay in bed and wake up. This is a good time to pray or repeat affirmations, or plan your day
- Drink a glass or two of water; preferably room temperature. Something warm is best because it helps move toxins through the system. Warm water with lemon juice is good
- empty your bowels and bladder

- clean your tongue (metal tongue cleaners or toothbrushes work)
- use mouthwash or oil to swish and remove bacteria and toxins that accumulate overnight (oil actually pulls toxins from your mouth; coconut oil works good; this promotes healthy gums and teeth)
- Brush your teeth
- Wash your face and clean your eyes. Also removing mucus from your nose cleans your nasal passages. You can use a neti pot and a little bit of oil just on the tip of your pinky finger to keep the nostrils lubricated and healthy; the neti pot can be used as you can tolerate it, some people like it daily, some once a week. This can help prevent respiratory issues, colds, sinus headaches, congestion and allergies. It can assist breathing and reduce snoring, too.
- During the morning quiet time and before the distractions of the day begin, is the best time to meditate or pray. This is also a great time to spend just five minutes practicing breathing exercises. We will talk more about meditation in another chapter, but morning is the best time to meditate.
- Exercise: we will cover what exercise is best for which dosha in a following chapter. You don't need to exercise for more than 20 or 30 minutes a day, but movement is important.
- Do a dry brush massage on your skin. This can be accomplished with a natural fiber brush, bath gloves, Garshana gloves, or a very light loofah. You don't want to damage your skin, you just want to lightly buff off the dead skin. Start at the feet and ankles, then legs, then arms, then hips and core. You can use a brush to reach your

back. Don't buff your heart area. Buff up and down up to 20 times in each place, and buff in circles over your joint areas. Don't brush too harshly, but do use a rapid motion. You have a layer of lymph fluid under your skin and buffing your skin stimulates your immune system and circulation, and it detoxifies. Don't forget your scalp! Bend over and vigorously massage your scalp with your fingertips. When you are done, massage a light layer of oil all over your skin. Let it sit for no more than 15 minutes and then shower or bathe. Oiling is a pulling tool that pulls toxins out of our skin. If you leave it on too long, your skin will become dry and somewhat crepey because the oil starts to pull the natural fluids, also. Lukewarm water is best. You only need soap where soap is needed, and your skin will be smooth and shiny, glowing with good health. We eliminate toxins through stool, urine and sweat, so when you take care of your skin your ability to detox works even better. You can use warm oil on your scalp, too. If you have short hair and want to leave a little oil in for a sheen, that's great! If you have long hair and don't want that kind of mess, try and do this once a week. Also, putting shampoo on your hair while it is still dry, will help to emulsify and draw the oil out. Just let it sit for a couple of minutes before you rinse out the shampoo and oil. We will cover more about oils in a following chapter.

+ Eat breakfast, but only eat if you are hungry. Your body will let you know so listen to your gut!

+ Your largest meal should be between 10am and 2pm. This is when the Sun is highest in the sky and when your digestive juices are at their peak. If you can, walk around or move for 5 to 15 minutes after eating. This allows your food to settle and creates serotonin in your system giving you a soothing, satisfied feeling.

+ Eat a light dinner. It's best not to eat after around 7pm. Leave at least 2 to 3 hours between dinner and going to bed to allow your body to digest the food (doing the dishes and minimal housework count; keep it light). Avoid any chaos around meal time and also mental activities or emotionally charged activities.

+ Avoid all electronics, including TV, cell phones, laptops, etc. at least an hour before bed, and none in bed! Take a warm shower or bath if you want (you can swap the morning skin buff and shower for evening if it fits into your schedule better). You can also do a self massage with soothing oils and essential oils before or after a bath or shower.

+ Drink something soothing like warm milk or tea (alcohol is a stimulant so for those of you who like wine right before bed, you are defeating the purpose).

+ Listen to soft music or read (a real book, not a Kindle) preferably something inspirational.

+ Spend 5-10 minutes recalling your day after you lay down and think about what you could have done differently; this is known as recapitulation.

+ Keep a pen and paper by your bed. If your mind is racing, write down your thoughts. Journaling can help get things out of your mind and onto paper and you can deal with them tomorrow.

- Close your eyes and just focus on your breath. Focus on any areas of tension or pain in your body and just purposefully relax those areas and breathe into them.
- Lights out no later than 10:30pm. Preferably go to bed around 10pm so you can try and be asleep by 10:30pm. This can be hard for some people who have developed habits over the years, but if you commit to creating new experiences, you can create new habits. Remember, this is what our biology is asking for!

Taking care of ourselves in the seasonal cycles is just as important as caring for ourselves through daily routines. The seasons can affect every cell in our body, and even our genes. When the seasons change our cravings for certain foods change, our moods change and our needs change. If we align ourselves with the dosha qualities of the seasons we can experience a greater sense of well being emotionally and physically. Again, we balance by applying opposites.

Seasonal cycles depend on where you live, but you get the point. The qualities will apply to the varying seasons in your area, and if you live in an area with a consistent climate, then even easier:

- mid-Summer/early Autumn - Pitta qualities: it gets hot!
- late Winter/Spring - Kapha qualities - wet/muddy, slowly waking up
- late Autumn/Winter - Vata qualities - getting dry and windy

Seasonal routines (do the best you can; if the seasons vary where you live, then apply the opposite characteristic to that season):

+ Mid-Summer/early Autumn - choose cool, light foods and beverages. Salads, smoothies, and sandwiches can provide light fruits and vegetables with plenty of moisture. Avoid getting overheated and focus on cooling, calming activities like swimming or taking walks early morning or late evening. Avoid the midday heat. Wear light fabric, cooling clothing. Since this season has Pitta qualities, Pitta people need to stay cool, hydrate with cool beverages, eat cooling foods, and stay inside so they don't have a meltdown! Kapha people enjoy warm weather and have the stamina to go all day, even if it's very slow. Vata people also enjoy warm weather; but they have a hard time sleeping and with longer days it makes it even harder for them.

+ Late Winter/Spring - choose lighter, warmer foods with spices like rice bowls or stir frys, or ethnic type foods with lots of spice and flavor that aren't too heavy (think Tacos!). Try to get outside to perform exercise to counteract the heavy, wet feeling of spring and breathe the fresh new air. Wear clothing that keeps you dry and warm. Try to sleep a little less to enjoy the longer light during the day (but still try to aim for 6-8 hours per night). Don't take naps! Kapha people need to try not to sleep too much during this time, and they need to stay warm, but try to get outside and move. Pitta people love the cooler weather, especially the rain, and can eat what they want most of the time, but need to beware of too much spice, peppers, and pungent foods in their diet; it stokes their fire! Vata people need to stay very warm during this time, and need to strive to get plenty of rest (sleep a little longer) and savor flavorful foods.

+ Late Autumn/Winter - choose lightly cooked, warm and heavy, moist foods like casseroles, soups, stews. Get plenty of rest. It gets dark earlier so go to bed a little earlier. Drink plenty of fluids and choose comfortable, warm clothing. Good idea to exercise indoors during this season. Vata people need to eat heavy, moist, cooked, grounding comfort foods during this time, and definitely stay warm, and take naps if necessary. Pitta people need to eat but stay active and sweatshirts usually keep them warm enough during this season. Kapha people need to really watch what they eat during this time of year, and stay on the lighter side with soups in place of stew, and light protein like fish or chicken, and lots of vegetables!

Because we change the way we eat and dress and feel from season to season, it is a good idea to cleanse between seasons. Detoxing or cleansing during the Equinoxes and Solstices is a good idea to transition from one season to the next.

Fasting for 24-36 hours, or doing a cleansing of your choice is a good way to enhance elimination and digestion. Usually one day is all it takes (24 hours). If you are a person who is interested in trying a 36 hour type fast, as an example, you would start at 7pm Sunday night and eat again at 7am Tuesday morning.

Another fasting option is doing a slow cleanse over seven days. This is a wonderful way to feel rejuvenated and joyful, and a little lighter. You can use mild cleansing herbs and eat breakfast and your midday meal, but skip the third meal of the day. If you get hungry and don't think you can miss the third meal, eat something very light; maybe a soothing fruit, but something very simple. Eating lightly cooked, easily digestible foods like oatmeal, rice, sweet potatoes, soups and soothing spices helps your body carry out toxins without stress. This is the time to eat foods that are not too filling, and meat is not recommended. This is a time when you can just eat two smaller meals with filling grains, beans or legumes and other tasty foods, to slowly transition from one season to the next. One bowl dishes like soup, kitchari, light stews, beans and rice, or stir fry type dishes are great for this type of cleanse. Stick to whole foods and cook both meals. This is a week full of high fiber prebiotic foods. This is somewhat similar to intermittent fasting, as you have about 16 hours between the midday meal and the following morning meal. You will find that at the end of the week you feel amazing. Sometimes during this type of fast, or any other type, you will experience flu-like symptoms or just feeling a little ill after 2 or 3 days. This is just your body dealing with the junk, but after the 4th or 5th day, you will begin to notice a beautiful change.

Simply eliminating solid food for a day, or juice fasting, or just eating soup can be a simple way to cleanse. Also, completely eliminate processed, fried and canned foods from your diet during a transition (maybe permanently!). If you need a little boost in the beginning, the Castor Oil your Grandma used still works in light doses (a Tablespoon or less), and Senna is strongly recommended. Senna is a natural plant product that works very gently and works with the body's own fluids. Fasting can make you feel lighter and it doesn't take long for your body to take care of all the garbage and clean up! You'll feel better for it. Not everyone wants to fast and not everyone can fast. Make sure you check with your medical professional before proceeding with a fast so you don't compromise or compound any medical issues you have.

Massage therapy during this kind of "lightening up" can be very healing and also help to move toxins through your system. There are a variety of massage types, and even acupuncture can assist with detoxing. Other healing modalities like marma point therapy and panchakarma can assist in making rapid, holistic changes to your physiology that create higher levels of consciousness in a very short time. Another great way if you have access, is to use a sauna to really sweat everything out. In Native America the sweat lodge ceremony is indicative of a new birth. The lodge itself represents the womb and you enter the lodge on your knees and to the left. Cedar or other plants are used on the hot rocks to promote healing, and water is thrown on the rocks periodically during the process to create steam. The sweat is profuse and profound, along with the singing and drumming. Just fasting for a period of 24 hours and using a sauna can create a radical change in your body, mind and spirit! Coming out of the lodge is a new birth and what happens in the lodge is left there for the healing environment to deal with. The sweat lodge is a lot like a confessional; what is said there and what happens there, is left there. Some who have experienced great trauma can get very emotional or very sick, and the confines of the lodge and the fire clean up all that for you. The steam draws all the negative out of your body, and the smoke cleanses your extended body and carries it all away. You have to make sure you drink lots of water and stay hydrated if you make a decision to fast and use a sauna. Water is energy and the fluidity of it connects us to the fluid nature of the universe.

If you have any kind of propensity toward an eating disorder, do not attempt a fast or any change in your diet without the advice of your medical professional. Eating disorders can be especially hard to treat because we need food to survive and food is the drug of choice with an eating disorder.

Even the stages of our life have dosha qualities. From birth until about our late 20's or mid-30's we are in a Kapha period. Kapha is all about structure, foundation and security as the water and earth dosha. We are growing and learning; we laugh a lot and we tend to play a lot. We are loved and we are loveable during this stage. Then from the end of that Kapha period until we are in our late 40's to mid 50's we are in a Pitta period of our lives. Pitta is all about transformation and we are working and creating our lives and transforming as an adult, independent of our youth. The final stage of our life is a Vata period when we begin to get a little more frail, anxiety and worry kind of invade our space more than usual during this time. Vata is all about movement and we become lighter and airy during this stage, we are quick to change our thoughts, and our digestion becomes variable. The Vata time of our life is a ripe time for imbalances based on the accumulation of our past, especially mentally if we have not properly digested our issues. If we can learn to take better care of ourselves in our youth and through our middle ages, what a wonderful time Vata could be. We have accumulated a lot of experience and wisdom by then, and what a wonderful time in our life to share it. Sometimes creativity during this period can be a great way to balance, and act as a distraction to the worry and anxiety.

# CHAPTER SIX:

## *Step Three: Eating Right*

*E*ating is one of the best ways to balance every dosha type; we are what we eat, literally! Eating is also one of the easiest ways to throw a dosha out of balance. In our fast moving world we tend to eat far too much processed food, and eat on the run. We also eat at the wrong times and over eat or under eat. How we eat is just as important as when and what we eat.

What we eat is important because our gut health is extremely important; 70-80% of our immune cells are present in the gut. That should make you think twice about what you put in your mouth, what ends up in your gut, and how that affects your immune system! The better we take care of our gut health, the stronger and more able our immune system will be to defend us.

The microbiome of our gut is a community of microbes, such as bacteria and other organisms, that fight for and maintain our health. Diversity relates to the number of individual types of bacteria and microorganisms from each species that reside in our gut, and richness relates to the total number of each bacterial species in the total microbiome. It's super important to maintain both for optimum digestion and health! We need to properly feed this community in our gut so the richness and diversity are stable, and so that nutrition can be delivered elsewhere in our system and keep us vibrantly healthy. Having a low diversity of microbiome in our gut can lead to a variety of chronic illnesses including diabetes, high cholesterol, insulin resistance, obesity, colon cancer and other colon issues like colitis, celiac disease, allergies, chronic fatigue syndrome and many others. So, how do we maintain our gut health? We feed it right. Antibiotics are really useful in treating bacteria and infections. However, one round of antibiotics can really mess with your gut flora. Ask your doctor if it is okay to take a probiotic while you are taking antibiotics.

Probiotics are good, live bacteria and/or yeast that live in your gut and help keep you healthy. They work in your favor when you have bad bacteria, like an infection, that has entered your system. They also help your body by supporting your immune system and controlling inflammation, making vitamins and breaking down medications. Prebiotics are a food source for the microorganisms in your gut. The probiotics and prebiotics work together and eventually make their way to the colon doing all kinds of interesting work along the way. Prebiotics are fibrous foods like grains, fruits, vegetables, and legumes and should be eaten everyday. Probiotics are fermented foods and supplements that can help boost and maintain levels of good microbes in your gut. There are a lot of good quality probiotic supplements to choose from, and probiotic foods include yogurt, kefir, sauerkraut, pickles, kombucha and kimchi, just to name a few. Probiotics should also be taken everyday. Because so much of our immune system is in the lining of our gut, this helps keep every system in our body healthier by helping to maintain the richness and diversity of our gut colony.

When we eat right we have more energy, toxins are dispelled easier and our body systems operate efficiently. This good health shines from the inside out and gives us more useful energy. When we don't eat right we experience illness, sluggishness, foggy thinking, depression, inflammation, weight gain and a host of other malicious issues.

Avoiding processed foods and eating whole foods is best. Processed foods are anything that comes in a can, a box, a bag or a package. An exception to this, as an example, are bagged fruits or vegetables that are frozen. Also organic foods that have not been processed, like quinoa or rice. You have to use your common sense here, and read the labels. Processed foods tend to have a lot of fat, sugars, salt, and preservatives, depending on what they are, of course. Get in the habit of reading labels; I happen to like sardines that come in a can and provide a lot of good, healthy fats. Whole foods are foods in their raw or natural form, so fruits, vegetables, grains, nuts and seeds, legumes. Lightly cooked foods are favored over raw because they are easier to digest. That doesn't mean you can never eat raw foods, like a salad, or fruit, it just means that your body can more easily deal with lightly cooked foods. Fruit is really best eaten alone and if you're eating multiple fruits at the same time, it's best to eat fruits with similar qualities. As an example, peaches and pears have similar qualities, but bananas and pomegranates don't. Fruit is commonly eaten with cheese or cottage cheese, wine or yogurt, but think about what happens to the fruit in your stomach; the fruit will sour in your stomach. When you learn to really listen to your body, you can feel your food. You'll begin to understand on your own what food combinations feel good and which ones don't feel so good.

When we eat is important because our digestive system is strongest during midday when the sun is highest in the sky. We learned in the last chapter our main, or largest meal should be between 10am and 2pm because that's when our digestive juices are flowing. Kapha people tend to be sluggish in the morning due to the qualities of Kapha. Morning is a Kapha period of the day also, so then you have Kapha times 2. It's okay for a Kapha person to skip breakfast because when they're already sluggish during a sluggish time of day and then they add food, it just creates an even heavier feeling for them. If they do eat breakfast it should be light. Breakfast is a very important meal for Vata because of their light and airy nature, eating three square meals a day is important to ground them. However, it's very hard to get a Vata to sit and eat meals, so this is a practice in mindfulness for them; eating with intention. Pitta people are usually always hungry and can load up to get them through the day, as long as they are choosing the right foods. The evening meal for all three doshas should be smaller than the midday meal. The body is starting to slow down and prepare for a state of rest after around 6pm, and going to bed with food in your gut isn't recommended. Soup and salad, or something light is a good choice for this meal. Also, pay attention to the seasons and complement your biology. Snacking is not really recommended because if you're feeding your body right, you are getting what you need to nourish yourself, and you want to allow your body enough time to digest your food before you eat more. Pitta people have such an aggressive well functioning digestive system they often get hungry, so having a snack is recommended if they need it. Fruit, fresh or dried, is a great snack for Pitta. Otherwise, they start to get angry and irritable.

It takes about 3 - 5 hours for food to completely digest. You should allow your stomach the time to empty out before eating your next meal. We are very conditioned when it comes to food because of work, celebrations, time and other circumstances. We think we need to eat when it's noon because our employer says that's when we eat, or we think we need to eat at 6pm because that's what our parents said we should do when we were young. Many if not most of our life celebrations with family and friends are entirely based around food. These are times to be flexible and times to be enjoyed, but on a routine basis, how about eating when your body sends you signals that you're hungry?

A lot of people have huge issues eating food when they are not hungry because they tend to be emotional eaters. They eat when they're stressed out and they eat when they're thinking about something, or even if they're just bored. This is fog eating and just unconscious, unmindful stuffing something in your mouth. This happens a lot when people are sitting in front of the television or working on a computer! In a previous chapter we learned about chronic stress and stress hormones that can cause inflammation and other issues. When we eat while we are experiencing stress, stress hormones like cortisol and adrenaline are being excreted and our body wants to deal with the stress first. The food gets stored away as fat or reserves so after the body has a chance to calm down then it will go back and breakdown the storage and do what needs to be done. But when we are exposing ourselves to repeated stress by racing thoughts, worry, anxiety, or internal and external environmental issues, that fat and unhealthy fog food kind of begins to be the norm. Eventually ill health and disease manifest as a result of our body not being given the opportunity to deal with the nourishment on an optimum level.

Strive for 2 or 3 meals a day and little to no snacking, with the largest meal in the middle of the day. There are a lot of physical fitness programs that recommend eating 6 meals a day at 2 ½-3 hour intervals, including post workout meals, and 10pm meals. These programs also recommend drinking a specific number of glasses of water per day. Your body will let you know when you are thirsty and hungry if you listen to it. Vata people have a dry quality to them anyway, and they should hydrate frequently. Kapha people carry a lot of water as a normal trait of their body type, and they probably don't need to drink as much water as other body types. Pitta people are a combination of fire and water and drinking too much water can cause their fire to turn to steam and then turn to embers. There is no one size fits all fitness program. We need to understand who we are and what's best for our essential nature in order to keep it in balance and live harmoniously with Mother Nature. Also, be careful not to make the mistake of thinking physical fitness is equal to health. We certainly need to move our body and we gain a lot of benefit from exercise and mindful movement. However, it is only one component of health. If we are stressed out or stressing our body and forcing it into submission by doing activities we don't enjoy or activities that aren't good for us, we are defeating the purpose and risking injury.

Addiction manifests in all sorts of different ways and getting addicted to, or being addicted to fitness activity is a real thing. Food addiction and eating disorders are a serious, life threatening matter that require intervention and medical attention, so err on the side of reason if you're dealing with, or are someone with this kind of issue.

How we eat is as important, if not more important, than what we eat and when we eat. Eating is a sacred, self-nurturing act of providing nourishment to our body. When we create an environment of contentment and calm when we eat, our body hormones are stable and are ready to work in our favor. It is important to be grateful for food regardless of the quality or the access to it. Preparing a meal and sitting down to pay attention to the food, and savor the food is extremely important to our biology and the way our food gets digested. Some people eat luxuriously and some people may only be able to afford a little bit, or food of less quality. Whatever situation you are in, hopefully you can express your gratitude for what you have and spend the few minutes it takes to enjoy what you have. Your body will thank you for it! Setting a table with a single flower in a vase, or a candle, or a picture can make a difference. Turning on some music you like also sets a great mood. Sharing food with family and friends can also create an atmosphere of joy. You are probably better off enjoying a cheeseburger and fries instead of a salad if you are in the right mindset and in the right emotional state. Just being aware while you're eating and focusing on the food actually helps your brain tell you when you are full. Focus on each bite one at a time. Put your fork down or put your food down after each bite. Chew and focus on the flavor, the appearance, the textures and the way it makes you feel when it hits your gut. Focus on chewing and making sure you are chewing and swallowing an entire bite before you put more in your mouth. Take the time to honor the food and honor the fact that it is nourishing every cell in your body.

Sometimes this advice is hard, but old food is dead food. Food shouldn't be kept for more than two days unless you freeze it and reheat it later. We use microwaves routinely these days, but sometimes they can compromise the nutrition in food. Do your best with what you have to work with and make sure you're feeding yourself to the best of your ability. Eating can be a very grounding activity if we do it right, and we can feel the nourishment flowing through our body if we pay attention. It's nice to be able to get up and move for 5 or 10 minutes after eating a meal, also, just to let everything settle.

One of the most powerful exercises you can engage in is eating an entire meal in complete silence. This can be very hard if you have a house full of family, especially young kids! But, if you can manage it, try and find a place or carve out some space for you to fix an aesthetically pleasing, and flavorful meal and just be in the moment as you take it in. Just eating in mindfulness without speaking can be an extremely powerful form of meditation and give us a small glimpse into the spiritual aspect of feeding our body. When I was struggling to create my own space and step away from the struggles in my marriage, and heal myself, this is one of the first ways I accomplished that. I would sometimes take myself out to dinner and a movie, or just out to dinner. It's a powerful thing to eat alone and just be in the moment without any distractions. I came to really enjoy that time alone and just ate slowly, savoring every bite with nowhere to be and no one to bother me. It gave me a sense of control and independence, and sort of freedom, to be nurturing and caring for myself like that.

It isn't necessary to remove anything from your diet if you are sticking to whole foods; unless of course you have food allergies. This seems to be getting more and more common. If you need to stay away from certain foods due to allergies, there are plenty of alternatives these days! Fruits and vegetables have a different type of sugar than processed sugar, and nuts, seeds, avocados and other natural healthy fat sources have a different type of fat than processed fats. If you have a sweet tooth, try replacing processed sugar with pure maple syrup, agave syrup, monkfruit, sweet fruit juices, dried fruits like dates, molasses or honey. If you have gluten issues try almond, coconut, potato or garbanzo bean flour. Use your imagination and use your spices and herbs!

Kapha people are naturally larger boned, with a sturdy, structural frame, they are usually muscular and have a little extra layer of fat on their frame. Sometimes these are the people who are desperate to lose weight and can't! This is their natural state and because their qualities are thick, sticky, dense, solid, smooth, slow, heavy, when they attempt a low carb diet it can be a disaster. Think about the quality of foods on a low carb diet. Usually it is meat, nuts and seeds, cheese, avocados and vegetables. The vegetables, great!!, but the rest of the foods have the same qualities of Kapha that the Kapha person has! More of the same just increases the Kapha and sends the Kapha person into an imbalance of heaviness, lethargy and sluggishness. You can be imbalanced, remember, either by not having enough of your essential nature, or having too much. Pitta people can't eat a lot of hot foods or sour foods on a routine basis, because they already have such a fire burning bright in their digestive system, these foods just stoke the flame even higher. Imagine a Pitta person sitting outside in the hottest time of the year, during the hottest part of the day, drinking alcohol. It would be like a volcano nearly ready to erupt. And rest assured, with all that heat they will erupt, and you probably don't want to be anywhere near them when that happens! Vata people are light, airy, quick, spacy, dry, and whimsical. What happens if a Vata person eats nothing but rice cakes?? Their Vata increases because the rice cakes have the same Vata qualities as the Vata person. Unfortunately, for the Pitta and Kapha, ice cream and pie can actually be very grounding for a Vata person. They need foods with the opposite quality of their dosha to ground them. These would be foods with Kapha qualities of thick, sticky, heavy dense, smooth (think peanut butter!).

If you aren't confused enough by now, we are going to go even deeper. This is the secret to balancing your dosha with food. Food is medicinal, food is nourishing, food is sacred and good food is important. Food can either heal you or it can kill you; food is medicine and medicine is food. So many times I've seen at the grocery store someone on a scooter with several cases of soda pop. Just think about the stress all that sugar, sodium and carbonation put on your body, and with zero nutritional benefit! It's just so incredibly sad what we do to our bodies with food. It affects everything about us including our sleep, our digestion and our overall sense of well being.

Foods, including herbs and spices, fall into six categories of taste. These tastes are very powerful and therapeutic. So much so that they can influence our moods, our physiology, our state of mind and our consciousness. Foods also have qualities just like the doshas. In order to keep our dosha in balance, we eat foods that are opposite qualities of our dosha, why? Because opposites balance one another, and like increases like (yes, that's worth repeating again).

Remember when determining the dosha, most people are a combination of two doshas. However, everyone has a little bit of all three doshas in their nature. This is simply because digestion is a Pitta function, but everyone has it, Vata is an air and movement function, and Kapha is our structural system like bones, for example. The quizzes we mentioned in Chapter 4 are used to determine your dosha type, and the various combinations of the doshas were discussed. Let's say for example, the first quiz you completed showed that you were a Vata-Pitta combination. This would indicate that Vata is your primary dosha and Pitta is your sub-dosha and you have very low Kapha qualities. Vata's are naturally small framed, thin or slender by nature, light and airy, so if a Vata is overweight or carrying a little extra fat, that would be a Kapha imbalance. If a Vata has a stomach ulcer, indigestion or skin rash, that is too much heat and would be considered a Pitta imbalance. If a Pitta person is experiencing excessive worry and anxiety, this is a Vata imbalance and they could focus on more grounding foods until they feel like they've come back to balance. This can get complicated if you put too much focus on analyzing it instead of focusing more on how you feel. If you have a fair idea of the qualities of each type of dosha, then you will begin to notice the slightest bit of imbalance in your system, and you can gently work to bring it back into balance.

The six categories of food are:

Sweet, salty, sour, pungent, astringent, bitter
All six tastes should be included in every meal.

Each dosha has three primary tastes that keep their dosha in balance, so should have more of those tastes included in their meal, but should include all six. The reason we include all six is because they work to tell our brain that we are satiated. We eat a meal including all six tastes, and eat until we are about 70-80% full and then we stop. This leaves room for our food to digest and instead of stuffing our face until we feel sick, we are at an optimum level to give our body the space to do its work. Our stomach is designed to hold approximately 4 cups of food. When too much food is put into it, it stretches and expands the gut and then we feel nauseous. It's best not to drink when you eat. It's especially important not to drink iced liquids when you eat because cold drinks stop the digestive process. Warm drinks in small quantities are okay. Another good indicator is when you feel more thirsty than hungry, stop eating. Drinking a glass of water a few minutes before a meal is another way to take up space so you don't over eat.

Vata should concentrate on mostly: Sweet, sour, salty
Pitta should concentrate on mostly, Sweet, astringent, bitter
Kapha should concentrate on mostly: Astringent, pungent, bitter

Not only do foods fall into these categories, but so do herbs and spices. Herbs and spices are a great way to incorporate some of the tastes into your meal, and they are medicine for your gut! As an example, turmeric reduces inflammation and has a whole host of other health benefits. Coriander, fennel, black pepper, cinnamon, nutmeg and clove are all considered to be carminative herbs and soothe and relieve pain in the stomach, and reduce flatulence. Including some of these spices when you're cooking beans or cruciferous vegetables like broccoli and cauliflower, can help stop gas before it starts.

Ginger is great for gut health and you can just chew on a piece of raw ginger or make a tea from ginger root and just sip it during the day. It's a good way to spice up dishes without making them too hot.

*Sweet foods* include meat, dairy, grains, fats, sugars, honey, molasses, maple syrup, agave, pasta, rice, and breads. Sweet foods are made of water and earth, and are soothing.

*Sour foods* are pretty obvious; lemons, yogurt, pickles, vinegar, and certain citrus fruits. Sour foods are a good way to enhance stomach acids if you have a sluggish system and need a pickup. Sour foods are made up of earth and fire qualities.

*Salty foods* are salt, and foods that have a lot of salt added. Salt has water and fire elements.

*Pungent foods* are certain spices like cloves and ginger, and salsas, radishes, hot peppers, horseradish, onions, garlic, mustard. These can really improve your digestion and add fire if you have digestive issues. Sometimes these foods can even cause you to sweat and release toxins from your system, and they can give your metabolism a boost. These foods have air and fire qualities.

*Astringent foods* are foods that can make you pucker. Tea, coffee, tart fruits, beans, cranberries, pomegranates, cauliflower, some citrus fruits, some berries, red wine all have astringent properties. These foods have earth and air qualities

*Bitter tastes* include all the leafy greens, sprouts, beets, broccoli, celery and many others. These are very good for detoxifying and promote weight loss. These foods have air and space qualities.

Lots of foods have more than one quality. As an example, oranges sometimes can be sweet, but also sour, and can also have an astringent quality to them; apples also. Peanuts are a legume and can be salty and astringent. Kiwis can be sweet and sour, and also astringent. Peppers can be sweet and pungent at the same time. Lightly cooking some foods changes the qualities. Onions are a good example of this. They are very pungent and bitter when raw, but when they are caramelized they take on a sweet quality.

Some examples of how you might include all six tastes in your food could be:

Oatmeal with cinnamon, nutmeg, a tablespoon of nuts and seeds, raisins, a pinch of salt, a pinch of black pepper, pure maple syrup for sweetener, and maybe an orange or grapefruit.

Think ethnic foods! A lot of ethnic foods include all six tastes in every dish they serve. Mexican food includes beans and rice (astringent and sweet), salsa (bitter, pungent, sour) and cheese (salty; sometimes sweet, pungent or sour depending on the cheese).

Stir fry, casseroles, stews and soups, smoothies, salads and sandwiches are another great way to include all six tastes.

If you're like me and like a little sweet treat after a meal, use your imagination and try dates or raisins, sweet cherries, or rice pudding. I love to make stewed apples with lots of spices and pure maple syrup for sweetener, then mix oatmeal, brown sugar, butter and flour on top and bake like a crisp. A little heavy cream on top doesn't hurt either.

You don't have to eat a lot to include all six tastes, you just have to be a little creative. Have some fun with this, and lightly cooking herbs and spices that you include can really bring out the aroma and flavor of a dish. The whole purpose of this is to care for yourself, and to heal!

So many colors are available in the produce section, too! It is really important to eat the rainbow! Foods that have the same color have the same nutrients, also. Be sure and include these to make your meal beautiful!

Red foods are a good source of lycopene and capsanthin. Think tomatoes, all the red berries, peppers, grapes and cherries, apples, tomatoes, chard and cabbage.

Orange and yellow foods are good sources of beta-carotene, beta-cryptoxanthin and flavonoids. These include squash, lots of different types of fruits, yams, pumpkin, peppers, carrots, and corn.

Eat your greens! These are a good source of lutein and chlorophyll. Lots of fruits and vegetables fall into the green category! Chard, arugula, lettuce, peas, zucchini, celery, avocados, apples, grapes, kiwi, limes, spinach, kale, and more.

Purple (sometimes dark blue) foods are a good source of anthocyanins and phenolic acid. These are full of flavor and include plums, certain berries, blue corn, blue potatoes, cabbage and eggplant.

White foods are a great source of allicin and flavonols. These include coconut, pears, onions, garlic, potatoes, cauliflower and others.

You don't need to know all of the phytonutrients in every plant, just pick the colors and mix them up! Hopefully you can see now how you don't need to spend a lot to eat well. Especially if you are sticking to just two or three meals a day as you should, preparing and cooking your own food, and taking better care of yourself. When we eat our fruits and vegetables, our nuts and seeds, our grains, our beans and legumes, and our spices and herbs we combine a lot of different types of phytonutrients that keep us in balance and healthy. Many, many ailments can be prevented and even cured if we eat the right foods and make sure we are giving our body what it needs and not just what we want!

You don't have to give up anything, and you will find that the flavor of your food is even grander than something out of a box or a drive-thru window. Some people remove things from their diet like dairy, caffeine, gluten, sugar, etc. This is an entirely personal choice because everyone has a unique biology and what one person can tolerate, another cannot.

# CHAPTER SEVEN:

## *Step Four: Exercising Right*

*E*ating right, sleeping right and exercising right have to be part of our daily routine if we want to focus on nurturing ourselves first, and if we want to experience optimum health. It is the body, mind and spirit we are effectively trying to reharmonize to create a holistic internal environment so we can respond differently and create change in our external environment. It's pretty easy to raise an arm or a leg by just thinking about it. It isn't too difficult to control your breath by just thinking about it, but can be slightly difficult if you've been running and are huffing and puffing. But, it's very difficult to try and control our runaway mind and all the thoughts we have. When we find the exercise that is right for our essential nature, we not only invoke balance, but we can also bring together the body, the breath and the mind. Of course this takes a fair amount of focus, but part of the creation of a daily routine is creating stability and mindfulness, and we should apply mindfulness to everything we do. If we pay attention to our body when we are exercising, and move in a mindful manner, we can focus our breath on each movement and into areas of our body where we need strength to complete or continue the motion.

Each of these activities we are learning, ground us and give us an opportunity to focus on one activity at a time. This can be very healing and soothing. Also, as a recap, each step of each of these principles is intended to begin the physical healing process, that leads to the mental healing process, that leads to the spiritual or faith based healing process. When our mind is wrought with worry and our body is shackled by stress it can be hard to do the right thing. So, if we create a daily routine eventually we don't have to try so hard to take good care of ourselves; it will begin to come naturally, and happen second nature. The creation of new habits happens gently and easily if we are consistent and persistent in our application, and eventually the bad habits are just replaced and fall by the wayside, and we won't miss them at all.

There are a wealth of benefits to cardiovascular exercise, and it should be included in our schedule at least three times a week for 20-30 minutes. Some people like to work out in an environment that motivates them, like a gym or fitness center. Others like peace and quiet, like to be alone, or like the outdoors. It doesn't matter what method you choose because yard work, house work, hiking, all count just as much as an elliptical, treadmill or rowing machine. Don't try and force yourself to do something you hate or it becomes hard to stick with it. Find something you enjoy and make it part of your healing practice.

I walk my dogs every single day with few exceptions. Somebody has to die or be sick for me to miss my walk. I'm lucky to live in a rural area where I have room to move outside with few distractions. I walk anywhere from 1 ½ to 3 miles a day depending on the weather. I live in an area where we have four distinct seasons, so walking in the snow during winter months can be quite a chore! The ground I walk on is not entirely flat either, so I have a few small hills to hike up and down. I absolutely love the peace and quiet of the morning outside and to me it makes no difference if the sun is shining or if it's snowing or raining, I find beauty in every season. I find the beauty in every season because I choose to. I make it part of my practice to pray, repeat affirmations, chant mantras or sun gaze while I'm walking. It makes it more joyful for me and it keeps me in a state where I can enjoy the water as it slowly flows by, or watch the ducks as they swim by. I have a thing where I count geese when they fly overhead. Geese mate for life and if there is an odd number of geese in the gaggle, I always wonder if someone lost their mate. Taking deep breaths all the way into my belly and just filling it full clears my mind, my lungs and my heart! It really isn't about walking the dogs, it's about making the most of that moment of my life. It just feels joyful to be alive when I'm outside walking. Noticing everything around me with awareness and practicing mindfulness increases the pleasure.

If you have physical limitations, there are plenty of alternatives and adjustments you can make to ensure you are getting maximum benefit. Technology makes it very easy to exercise in any way we choose in our modern society. There are thousands of free videos we can choose from to learn new methods or enhance our old methods of exercise. As long as you are moving and moving with awareness, you are practicing mindfulness and getting maximum benefit. Just do something that allows you to enjoy the healthy boost! If you have limited mobility with your body, depending upon your limitations, breathing exercises are also a great way to exercise, especially if you can't move at all. Just bringing in the breath, holding it at the top of the breath for a few counts and then letting it go, then repeating, can be extremely rejuvenating and really get your circulation going.

Yoga is one practice that incorporates the body, the mind and the breath. There are a few different types of yoga, and it can be done in a flowing motion which provides a certain cardio benefit. It is also great for strength training, flexibility training and balance. This exercise can be good for every dosha type, and if you have issues, chair yoga is a good alternative. If you have joint issues or neck or back issues, swimming or water aerobics might be something you want to try to avoid any pressure on your joints or injury. Yoga practices include Hatha, Iyengar, Vinyasa, Ashtanga, and hot yoga. Whatever kind of exercise you choose, remember to keep it holistic and serve your body, mind and spirit while exercising.

In addition to doing some form of cardio two or three times a week, other forms of exercise should be done to increase muscle. This helps keep us young and strong. We lose muscle mass as we age at a rate of approximately 3-8% per decade after the age of 30. Literally, yikes! It doesn't take more than about 30 minutes of work in this form either. If we do 20 minutes of cardio exercise three times per week, that is only 60 minutes. If we incorporate 20-30 minutes of other types of exercise three times a week, that's another 60 minutes. That equates to two hours of exercise a week!

This doesn't have to be a grueling half day event that seems like a chore. Anywhere between 2 ½ to 4 hours a week is sufficient.

Since technology has increased in our lives, we tend to sit so often! Just get up and move. If you work at a computer most of the day, just make it a point to get up every hour and walk around for 5 minutes. Lots of people have jobs that are in construction or other areas that require constant movement. These people don't necessarily need to seek out additional exercise time, depending on their body type. Just as is with daily routines and with eating, the type of exercise you choose depends upon your dosha and keeping your essential nature in balance.

The very best time to exercise (for our biology) is in the morning. If you recall, from 6am-10am is a Kapha time of day when things are slow moving and kind of heavy. Exercise naturally picks up the pace and balances that Kapha time of day. Our schedules are all incredibly different, so do your best, and tune into your body to feel what seems best for you. If you are engaging your breath, your body and your mind together, as you should be, you'll know what feels best. It's almost always a bad idea to exercise close to bedtime because you get a little wound up and have a hard time falling asleep, unless you are practicing yoga, tai chi, Qigong or some other soothing activity.

Vata people are very active, light, quick people by nature. It isn't necessary for them to spend hours aggressively exercising. It tends to create more lightness and airiness about them and throws them off balance. Vata's need exercise that is balancing, slow moving and grounding. This might include activities like yoga, tai chi, leisurely walking, slow bicycling, light swimming, short hikes, Qigong, or even visualization.

Pitta people are generally athletic. They need a medium paced exercise routine that doesn't heat them up too much; hot yoga is a no-no for these people! Exercising outdoors is excellent for Pitta unless it's in the hot summer months. Skiing, swimming, a brisk walk, moderate hike, snowboarding, paced bicycling are all good exercises for Pitta; but never while the sun is highest in the sky.

Kapha people have a lot of strength and stamina. They are so easy going and naturally slow, they need a little boost to get their blood flowing. Aggressive exercise is best for these lovable people. They need to get the energy flowing by dancing, doing vigorous yoga, weight lifting, running, rowing, playing football or basketball where they run up and down the field or court. It's definitely best for Kapha people to exercise in the early morning because that is a Kapha time of day and they have a Kapha dosha which is two times the heaviness and sluggishness. They can be a lot of fun to exercise with because of their gentle and easy going nature.

Exercise will increase your desire to eat right and it will improve your sleep. Not only that, it will calm your mind and give you a little boost of serotonin, improve your memory and give you more energy. How can that be bad when we're trying to stay sane in an insane world!?

# CHAPTER EIGHT:

## *Step Five: Creating Harmony Within*

*A*ddiction is a merciless master. It turns a person you love into someone you don't know anymore, and someone they don't even know themselves. It makes it very difficult to express love in any grown up way, and quite often love comes out in the form of sobbing and tears, screaming and complete collapse. That's not love, it's heartbreak.

If you want love, you have to first learn to give love. Most addicts have lost the ability to really love, because their physiology has changed such that they do not have the physical, mental or spiritual capacity to even requite love. They absolutely have lost the ability to love themselves because of their shame and their inability to "fix" themselves. Many looking for love these days turn to internet search engines to be matched with someone who meets their expectations; they think if I can get these qualities in another human being then I will be in love. There becomes an entire tag list of items that some cyber individual should have, in order to be worthy of the lover. This is similar to what happens when we try to express our love to an addict, or they try to express theirs for us. The intention is there, but the conversation goes haywire because we end up telling each other how things need to be in order to have that love in place. When we tell someone we can only love them if they have a certain set of qualities or set expectations on that love, that is the lowest level of love.

But real love, particularly when we are talking about a higher love, is about loving another human being with compassion and empathy. It isn't about telling them if you do this, or if you have these qualities, then I will love you. We are talking about loving other human beings in spite of themselves. It has been my experience that most addicts are highly sensitive people and that becomes part of the problem, not the solution. They tend to feel so much and feel so deeply it just becomes sensory overload and they have to mask or numb their bad feelings or memories. Of course those bad feelings and memories increase the longer they are engaged in their addiction and the cycle just continues.

When I say the only way to love an addict is to love yourself first, that is the truth! What is the point of learning about a higher level of love only to make sure we direct that at someone else? We are just as worthy of that kind of love, aren't we? True love is a selfless gift. We cannot set criteria for the nature of a human being, and decide that if they meet all of the items on our list, only then will they be loveable, or deserving of our love. Instead, we have to start with our own qualities, see ourselves as loveable and use our own loving qualities for the sake of others. In that wave, true love will be returned exactly where and when it's necessary. Addicts, because of the shame and embarrassment caused by their addiction, suffer the lack of self worth to examine their loving qualities and their lovability. So, it's up to those of us who aren't under the influence or seeking the influence of an addiction, to make the necessary changes in our understanding of love.

When we've been living in a state of constant anxiety, stress, chaos, sleepless nights and worry, our mind is out of our control. It races with thoughts and false conversations that are never going to happen. We have all sorts of scripts and plays that take place in our head and then we latch on to them as believable; even though they never actually take place. We know now why sleeping, eating and creating daily routines are important to create mindfulness and healing, but we need to take these pragmatic, action steps one step further.

Recap: Pain is physical. When we are in pain we can take a pill or some kind of remedy to relieve the pain. Suffering is mental pain and takes place in the mind. The two aren't mutually exclusive, because one can cause the other, but alleviating suffering is much harder than alleviating pain.

We have to love ourselves first because if we don't we deplete all of our personal energy and we get depressed and we just don't want to try anymore. We end up just going through the motions of life making no difference at all; we are just existing. Our relationships with other people in our life can take a real beating too, because we are so focused on the person who is sick, we become sick ourselves. That's not terribly different from an addict; if we are addicted to thinking about them and addicted to all of the chaotic behavior that occurs on a routine basis then how do we distinguish between us and them?. Doing the same thing over and over gets you the same results, every single time.

So how do we stop? How do we change from a stressed out mess to a person who cares for and loves yourself and can then move up to higher ground?

We start by experiencing the world around us with our five senses. However, some things we experience are beyond our five senses. Between the two we can create a bridge to assist in our personal energy healing. We have our physical body and brain where all of our biological functions operate 24/7. But just outside of our physical body is a layer of energy that extends into our environment. New technology can measure this energy field and its responses, and we can tap into it to evoke healing in our physical body. You cannot see the wind, but you know that it is there. You cannot actually see the movement of the Moon as the lunar cycle proceeds, but you know that it is there. It doesn't appear to us that the Earth is constantly spinning, but we know that it is. You can't actually see the passing of time, yet you can feel it, and you know that it is there. You cannot see the bond that is immediately created between an infant and its parents when it is born, but it is undeniably there.

These things we have an inherent ability to know are created through life experience, and part of that experience are the functions of our five senses. Sight is associated with Pitta (transformational), taste and smell are associated with Kapha (structural and grounding), and sound and touch are associated with Vata (air and movement). To balance the mind we use smell, sight and sound, and to balance the body we use taste and touch.

When we need to get our mind under control, we might meditate or turn on soft music, or burn incense, or visualize laying on a beach or a nice forest scenery. We might also actually visit the beach and take in everything with all five of our senses. We can look at pictures, or picture scenes in our mind, and both are equally powerful. Our emotions are the accelerator for the balancing and our mind doesn't know the difference between whether we are actually there or if we are just visualizing it. To soothe and balance our body we can use food and the tastes we learned about (remember sweet is soothing, which can be dangerous if you love sugar!), or we can get a massage and experience a tender, gentle touch.

One of the reasons music is such a powerful force in our life is because it causes us to have emotions. We can remember all kinds of things in our life when we hear a certain song that we associate with that particular moment. Sound is a very powerful way to balance our mind. There are a variety of ways to use sound, music is the most obvious. Some people have a very soothing voice, and listening to audiobooks if you like the narrator's voice, can also help. Enjoyable sound affects our nervous system and our hormonal system, but sounds that we don't like also have an effect on those systems, but in the wrong way. These sounds actually have a physiological effect and either begin to heal us or cause stress responses. If your mind feels out of control, take some time to nurture yourself with sound. Mantras are sounds that are aligned with specific vibrations. They can be repeated over and over to create a vibration in your mind that is very beneficial. They do not have to be chanted or repeated out loud, this can be done in total silence with the same great benefit. This is a great way to distract your mind from racing thoughts and immediately calm down your physiology. Below are some ways to use sound to balance your mind, but get creative with what you love:

+ listening to sounds of nature, ocean waves, rain, wind, animals, birds
+ listening to music
+ chanting mantras
+ gregorian chants
+ drumming
+ singing bowls
+ chimes

Vata balancing with sound should be soothing, grounding sounds that are steady and low, or very warm and relaxing. Instrumental slow, mellow music or classical music (not upbeat) is an excellent way to balance Vata mind.

Pitta balancing with sound should be cooling, soft and sweet sounds. Sounds of nature are wonderful choices to balance Pitta, especially ocean waves, falling rain or running water. Flute music is also good for Pitta. A moderate tempo is good.

Kapha balancing with sound can be upbeat and invigorating. Rock and roll is a good choice for Kapha, or drumming or jazz. Something with a beat they can tap their feet to! It helps their sluggish system get up and go.

Another wonderful way to balance our mind is through sight. If you are a person who is able to visualize clearly, you may be able to balance your mind simply by closing your eyes and seeing internally. Looking at natural beauty has a profound healing effect on us. Some people prefer mountains and the forest, some oceans and the beaches, and others maybe animals and birds. Whatever it is for you, make sure you get more of it. Get out into nature if you can, and if you can't look at pictures of places that make you happy, then imagine yourself there. Even the simplest activity of decorating our home gives us an opportunity to add aesthetically pleasing things that give us pleasure when we look at them. These can include colors, statutes, pictures of our loved ones, plants and other items. The use of color when balancing with sight is very powerful! Even choosing specific colors for the clothes we wear can make a difference in our mood and in our balance.

Vata balancing with sight using colors would include earth tones and light pastel colors that are soothing, like gold or orange, or blue.

Pitta balancing with sight using colors would include cooling colors like green, aqua, soothing blues and even white.

Kapha balancing with sight using colors would include bold designs, shapes, geometric patterns and bright strong colors, like yellow, orange, red or gold..

Neuro Associative conditioning is a powerful way to train our brain! My grandmother used to bake bread all the time. I remember walking into her house and there was always something on the stove or in the oven. Those smells create emotions of love, security and nurturing in me; even now this many years later. When I bake bread it automatically makes me feel joy and I always think fondly of my Grandma. Smells can be a way to not only balance the mind but also to train the mind. Our sense of smell powerfully connects us to our instincts, our emotions and our memories and can trigger a healing response in our body. It can also help us to remember and keep us in line with our goals.

As an example, let's say that you use vanilla incense or burn a vanilla candle each time you read or take a warm bath. After a few times you will begin to associate the fragrance with the relaxing activity and it will trigger a sense of calm and relaxation in you, even before you read or take a bath.. Maybe you have a certain essential oil you use when you have a headache. Eventually, just the smell of that oil will cause your body to associate healing and pleasurable feelings, and you can likely get rid of a headache just through this association. You can use this method to set reminders for yourself, or just to relax in the moment, or to actually evoke a heightened state of well being, by just inhaling a fragrance that you have associated with an activity or a task.

Work with fragrances that you love and be creative. You can add a drop of essential oil to a body lotion or oil, maybe you can use a diffuser, a candle, incense, or even flowers or food! Aromatherapy is a powerful tool in our ability to kickstart a biological healing effect, so if there is something you want to be reminded of, or a task you want to make more enjoyable, use the power of smell to create a sense of peace before you start. Be consistent in this practice and before you know it, you will have trained your own body to respond positively to certain stimuli. If you have a goal or a project you are working on, use smell each time you start to work toward or on this goal or project. Eventually, this will trigger your consciousness to associate the two, and your work will be more enjoyable and more effective..

Smells to balance Vata should be sweet, floral, fruity and warm. Orange, clove, lavender, basil, and sour smells are good, too.

Smells to balance Pitta should be sweet and cooling. Fragrances like lavender, jasmine, mint, rose and sandalwood work well.

Smells to balance Kapha need to be stimulating and upbeat. Eucalyptus, clove, camphor, rosemary and juniper work well, along with other stronger smelling fragrances.

We talked about the power of taste in the last chapter. Balancing with food is a powerful tool! It's also, as was noted, one of the easiest ways to get us out of balance. It has everything to do with our emotions and our sense of well being, also our sense of security. To balance the doshas using taste, go back and review the information about the six tastes and which tastes to concentrate on for each dosha.

Touch is another great way to balance the body. Massage therapy of any kind is very nurturing, can stimulate the immune system, and help move toxins out of the system. Our skin is our largest organ and it releases toxins through sweat, and has literal mood altering peptides that respond to massage and touch. It's a literal dose of serotonin and dopamine that have similar effects as antidepressants. Touch is something we all need as human beings; without it we experience all kinds of psychological issues. Every dosha body can be balanced by a good strong hug! Even a self massage before or after a bath, with an oil that's good for our dosha, can be a great way to calm our body and reinstate a sense of well being, and it's free! Spend a few minutes just rubbing your feet, your arms, your legs, any muscles that are tight or sore, and feel yourself relax.

Vata can be balanced through the power of touch using gentle, warming oils like almond or sesame, and prefer a soft, gentle massage.

Pitta can be balanced by using cooling oils such as coconut or sunflower. Pitta dosha prefers a soft, moderate touch massage.

Kapha can be balanced by a stimulating, deep tissue massage or method that is more aggressive. Balancing oils include stimulating smells like peppermint or eucalyptus.

Spending time in nature has an effect on all of our senses, including our sixth sense! We can take in everything and stimulate every sense. Just breathing in the fresh air and being, begins the healing process; we don't have to be doing anything at all. In fact, if we are just staring at a leaf, or watching the water roll by, or listening to the wind and the birds this becomes a form of meditation and we are immediately receiving the benefit. Being in nature and practicing focused listening, or sun gazing or laying on our back staring at the clouds is balancing the body, mind and spirit.

Being in nature is also one of the best places to process and release pent up emotions. Screaming and crying are both allowed and can be very liberating. If you have pent up energy, whether it's physical or emotional, placing your feet firmly on the Earth and then bending over and placing the palms of your hands on the earth. actually releases the energy into the ground.

Standing on the ground barefoot reduces free radicals. Multi-disciplinary research has revealed that electrically conductive contact of the human body with the surface of the Earth (grounding or Earthing, as it is known) produces intriguing effects on physiology and health. Such effects relate to inflammation, immune responses, wound healing, and prevention and treatment of chronic inflammatory and autoimmune diseases. We are connected to Mother Earth and all things on it, in it, around it, above it and below it. This grounding, or Earthing, reinforces that connection. It is imperative that we understand that the soil we walk on is responsible for our survival.

Our brain is our motherboard and processes all of the sensory information we take in. But our mind processes the information as an experience; it leaves an imprint like a footprint in the sand or the snow. Sometimes these imprints fade, but then come back as memories if we return to a place or recreate the same experience. There isn't any hard evidence to prove we've been there before, or had a certain experience, but we know. Some circumstances in our life are stronger than others because they are a result of our consciousness and these can literally affect our well being or physiology. One of the best examples of this are near death experiences. I actually had one of those when I was three years old.

I was at a babysitter's house and fell into the irrigation ditch. To this day, I can remember exactly what I was wearing, I remember how my hair was, I can remember being suspended in the water with my arms up over my head and just feeling very calm. Then I remember the babysitter's son plunging his arm into the water and pulling me up. I remember what he was wearing, too, but I don't remember anything at all about his face. He was probably around 10 years old, but when his arm plunged in to grab me, it was a grown man's arm with hair and large hands. I remember him pushing on my chest and I remember choking up water, and then shaking uncontrollably. I can remember sitting on the ground and the babysitter coming out and wrapping me in a blanket. She immediately took me into the house and made me a bowl of cereal (I can even remember what kind of cereal), but I didn't want to eat. I was crying and she sat me on the couch and called my mom. My mom left work and came to pick me up. I don't remember anything about what story was told to my mom or her reaction, and I don't remember anything after her picking me up, but years and years later when I recanted the story, my mom had no recollection. It was extremely traumatic for me and I believe I died for a few minutes that day. That imprint is more like an impression that I will never forget. It transcends my five senses and I have no explanation as a three year old child for remembering the arm of a man pulling me out of the water. I also have no explanation as to why I would remember exactly the clothes I was wearing or my hair, but it was as if I was watching me from somewhere else; from a more grownup viewpoint.

It seems to be the most traumatic events in our lives that we remember the most vividly; almost as if it just happened and we can remember every detail. This is because the experience, plus the extreme emotions involving the event just make it more powerful. But what about the joyful events in our life? These are also an experience and extreme emotions surround those, as well. A good example of this is the birth of a child. For most mothers, it's a day you never forget. Even though it is excruciatingly painful, the memory of the pain fades, but the birth of the child doesn't. We don't seem to relive the physical pain of childbirth over and over again, but we do relive the emotional pain of a traumatic event in our life over and over again. Remember, physical pain can be dulled with a remedy, emotional pain equals suffering, which is more in our mind. I have no scientific evidence to support this, but I think feelings are a physical sensation in our body created by our brain, and are a result of our emotions which are in the realm of the mind and our consciousness. We can feel love or hate from someone else just by being in the same room with them. It isn't necessary for them to touch us or even be close to us; we perceive these things through our sixth sense.

Let's say for example, you go to the doctor and get a brain scan. The doctor is going to receive a picture of the actual physical mass of the brain and the colored areas of activity. During the brain scan the doctor asks you to picture in your mind your mother's face, and maybe her address. Is the doctor going to see your mother's face on the brain scan, or are they going to be able to see the numbers associated with your mother's address, or a picture of her home? The answer is obviously no. However, they will see certain areas of your brain light up as the recall activity processes and the colors brighten or dull.

"The Axis of Knowledge" runs vertically through the center of our bodies, through the pineal gland located in the exact center of the brain, running vertically through our heart and solar plexus (the Y Axis). Another line runs horizontally through the prefrontal cortex of the brain (the first X Axis), and intersects through the pineal gland. This intersection connects our physical ability to see (one of our 5 physical senses), with the ability to see with our mind's eye (one of our intuitive senses).

An additional X Axis, intersects with the Y Axis directly through our heart. This intersection connects the physical ability of the heart to pump blood through our veins with our emotional ability to feel love and sadness in our heart.

A third X Axis, intersects with the Y Axis at the point of our solar plexus area. This intersection creates our ability to digest and dissolve waste and toxins, with our ability to sense danger or apprehension, or even excitement.

At each of the intersections of these axes occur real physiological and psychological connections. These areas are our "gut instinct" and "heartfelt" receptors, our instinctual and emotional indicators. The combination of the physical and psychological mechanics, creates our very human nature; our ability to bond and to reason, to think and to love. Each of these important intersections are little processors receiving and sending information in the energy field around and beyond us.

*Addiction tends to clog up or numb these physical and psychological receptor centers, and so does stress, worry and being out of balance. But there is still hope!*

## THE AXIS OF KNOWLEDGE

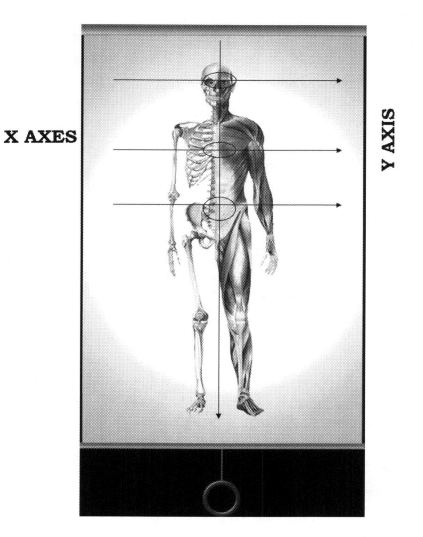

X AXES

Y AXIS

The chakra system of the body is similar, but much more intricate and sophisticated, than the intersections of our physical and psychological centers. It is part of the science of Ayurveda, and applying the techniques associated with the chakras is a powerful, energetic method of healing. Many energy healing practitioners use this system as part of their practice, but it is also something you can use on yourself. It is a wonderful way to pair your physical healing with your spiritual healing and growth. It is partly meditative and partly visualization. There are more than 7 chakras, but the system of 7 are the main chakras of the physical body and those are what we will work with. These chakras are energy centers that send and receive information and communication, and our life force runs through them. The energy of these centers or vortices, influences the health of our body, our mind, our spirit and our behavior.

The human brain is hailed as the most complex object in the universe and our power of thought appears to be unlimited. This can be exhibited by, for example, Olympic athletes who visualize every step of their routine in detail. Scientific studies have suggested that the body does not know the difference between perception and performing real events. When athletes picture themselves performing a routine in their mind, the same muscles trigger a response that would trigger if they were actually performing the routine. The imagination of the mind along with intention, is unquestionably the most powerful force in the universe. You can use this power of intention and visualization to tone your chakra centers. It is a lot like flipping on a light switch.

You can simply lay on your bed, in a bath, or wherever you feel comfortable to do a chakra toning. You can even sit in your car if that's someplace you can manage to be alone for a few minutes. It is a simple, yet profound process, of just focusing on the area, then focusing on the color, then silently repeating the mantra. You can listen to music while you are doing this, or drumming or chants, or binaural beats, or you can do it in complete silence. It entirely depends on you and what works for you. Some practitioners use crystal or metal singing bowls to do chakra toning. Each of the chakras is associated with a musical note in addition to colors and mantras, and the singing bowls are attuned to that note. There are a variety of videos and music on the internet that can help you on your chakra journey through guided meditations. Other practitioners use crystals or stones that correspond to the color of the chakra. The chakra stones can be placed over the chakra area or they can be placed in a circle around the person laying down. Experiment and find something that you are comfortable with, and then proceed.

To start with, identify maybe just one issue you are experiencing in your life, practice just focusing on the chakra associated with that issue. If it is physical pain, focus on that location. If it is emotional pain or confusion, focus on the chakra associated with that emotion. Focus on the area of the chakra, then fill that area with the color of the chakra, then silently repeat the mantra for that area, over and over. Be aware of any feelings, sensations, images or thoughts that occur. This exercise can create very powerful responses and emotions, and sometimes physical changes, so be prepared. It is best done alone where you can focus and not be disturbed, and where you can sit quietly for a few minutes when you are done to absorb the experience you've had. You will come to enjoy this and find it to be an effective, easy way to balance yourself. It can be long or short, it's entirely up to you.

The root chakra (Muladhara) sits at the base of your spine. It has a vortex that starts at the base of the spine and aims downward. This chakra color is red, and the mantra (vibration) is Lam (the "a" is pronounced as in awful), and the note is C. This chakra is associated with our basic needs, our sense of security, grounding and safety. This chakra can be compromised when your basic needs are not being met, including your emotional needs, or when you do not feel safe, secure or grounded. Imbalances in this area manifest as eating disorders, colon and bladder issues, lower back, legs and feet.

The sacral chakra (Svadhisthana) sits just between the top of the pubic bone and our naval. It has vortices that extend to the front and to the back. This chakra color is burnt orange, and the mantra is Vam (the "a" is pronounced as in awful), and the note is D. This chakra is associated with pleasure, creativity, and desire. This chakra can be compromised if our creativity has been stifled because someone told us we weren't good enough, or we don't think so ourselves. Reproductive issues or sexual abuse can also damage this area. It's important to create however we feel we can and not strive for perfection. It is the fun and the joy and the playfulness by which we create, not the process itself. Imbalances in this area manifest as addictions, depression, emotional issues, sexual dysfunction and a fear of change.

The solar plexus chakra (Manipura) sits in the center of our core, below our chest and above the naval. It has vortices that extend to the front and to the back. This chakra color is yellow, and the mantra is Ram (the "a" is pronounced as in awful), and the note is E. This chakra is associated with our personal power, self-confidence and capability. Imbalances in this chakra area include digestive issues, low self-esteem, anger or control issues, the inability to make decisions, loss of personal power, sluggish metabolism. This chakra in particular, can be balanced by applying the proper nutrition techniques outlined in a previous chapter.

The heart chakra (Anahata) sits in our chest area, from shoulder to shoulder. It has vortices that extend to the front and to the back. This chakra color is green, and the mantra is Yam (the "a" is pronounced as in about), and the note is F. This chakra is associated with love; we can send or receive love through this chakra center. Because this is our center of love, imbalances here will be opposite responses to love, including hatred, anger, fear or ignorance. A closed heart chakra can result in physical heart issues. Processing and letting go past hurts or heartbreak is a great way to balance this chakra also. Learning about a higher kind of love can also help. Volunteering or giving and practicing empathy and compassion can assist in raising the vibration of this chakra; when we help others, it makes us feel better too.

The throat chakra (Vishuddha) sits in the center of our throat area. It has vortices that extend to the front and to the back. This chakra color is blue, and the mantra is Ham (the "a" is pronounced as in about), and the note is G. This chakra is associated with our voice, our ability to speak our truth, and our communication. Imbalances in this chakra manifest as the inability to speak, the inability to express yourself or verbalize, lying, fear of speaking out, sore throat, thyroid issues. Always telling the truth and not being afraid to say what you mean and mean what you say, in a good way, are good ways to balance this chakra. So is singing or humming, and reading out loud to practice hearing your own voice.

The third eye chakra (Ajna) is in the center of our forehead. It has vortices that extend to the front and to the back, through the pineal gland. This chakra color is indigo, and the mantra is Sham (the "a" is pronounced as in awful), and the note is A. This chakra is associated with our intuition and our ability to see inward. Imbalances in this chakra manifest as the inability to trust your gut, doubt, limited vision or thinking, loss of trust in your sense of imagination, headaches, migraines. This area is in balance when we have imagination, intuition that is strong, visualization abilities, vivid dreams, a certain inner knowing. A strongly balanced third eye chakra can lead to telepathic and clairvoyant abilities to just "know" something. This is a spiritual chakra and having faith in something beyond our normal wisdom raises our vibration to a level above the normal day to day life we perceive through our five senses.

The crown chakra (Sahaswara) is at the center of the top of our head. This chakra has a vortex that extends from the top of our head upward. The chakra color is white or violet, and the mantra is Om (Ohm, or Aum), and the note is B. This chakra is associated with our connection to the universal source, Mother Nature, Spirit, Consciousness, our higher power, or God. It doesn't matter what you call it, this is an area of experience that transcends labels and human understanding.. This is a spiritual chakra and gives us the ability to transcend our human self. Toning this chakra, or activating this chakra can be done using prayer, meditation, sitting in silence and seeking spiritual connection. When we focus on this chakra we grow in awareness, become more compassionate, forgiving, kind and humble. We begin to have a stronger desire to serve others and live in a more conscious manner.

Repeat the mantra for each chakra and focus on the color until you feel a shift in that area. You are unique and if you are relaxed and focusing on the outcome and not the process, you will feel a shift. When you have finished the entire 7 chakras, visualize a healing, loving white light coming in through the crown of your head. Let it slowly billow down your head through the rest of your body, filling every area, every cell with healing, loving white light. Fill your whole body until you're full clear down to the tips of your toes. This white light is healing, protecting and filled with love and it knows where it needs to go. Let yourself come back to your own awareness slowly, and take some time to digest the experience.

The power of visualization is intense and amazing. You can make up your own visualizations and put yourself in a place or a state of mind you want to be in, just through the power of intention.

For physical pain, emotional suffering, or mental worry and anxiety, here is a very simple visualization you can practice. As you get better at it, you can develop your own using white light, or other colors of the chakras and see whatever negativity you have going on, just disappear! Simply picture yourself entering a bedroom and pulling a suitcase from under the bed. Everything you do not want in your life, you stuff into this suitcase. Watch yourself take each negative emotion, every feeling of anger and hatred, everything you don't want, and one by one put it into the suitcase. You fill it up until everything is in there. You can actually feel yourself get lighter as you shut the suitcase (you might have to sit on it) and zip it shut or lock the clamps, or whatever you have to do to lock everything inside. Then you take the suitcase outside, and you put it in a garbage bin, or you put it on a bus to be carried away, or you dispose of it however you see fit; maybe you light it on fire! However you do it, any pain, suffering, clutter, abuse, disease, literally everything negative, goes off with it. It is gone from your life. Picture yourself waving goodbye and finalizing by going back in the house and locking the door behind you. Picture your body filling with white light, a white healing light, that billows through your body from the top of your head to the bottom of your feet. This white light is picking up any residue left over, and it is healing any areas that need to be healed. Once your body is filled with white light just send the light to wherever it needs to go. Just focus on the light and feel its healing presence. The light knows what it needs to do and it knows when it is done. Thank yourself and spend a few quiet minutes loving yourself for this gift, and for making yourself feel better.

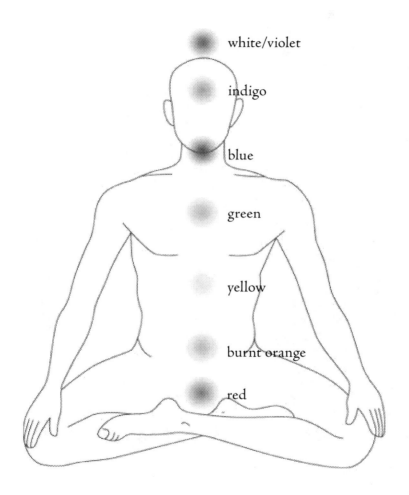

white/violet

indigo

blue

green

yellow

burnt orange

red

# CHAPTER NINE:

## *Step Six: Relief through Release*

*E*verything in our lives is about digestion, not just the food we eat. There are experiences we have when we see, feel or hear something that is somehow disturbing and that we cannot unsee, unfeel or unhear. It is so important that we have a way to digest these experiences, otherwise they end up as stuck emotions that we fixate on or obsess over. Violence and abuse trigger hormonal and physiological responses of extreme, acute stress and somehow we have to process that and then let it go. So many people spend years of their life, and sometimes an entire lifetime, clinging to traumatic experiences and paralyzed by the memory, and they are unable to move on. Even though there are times in life when happiness, joy and laughter are experienced, it is the looming trauma and sadness that hangs overhead like a giant shadow. When the abuse or violence continues over and over it feels impossible to make space to change directions.

The Kubler-Ross Model of the five stages of death was first introduced by Elisabeth Kubler-Ross in 1969. She was a Swiss born Psychiatrist who was a pioneer in studies of near death experiences. Her model identifies five distinct stages in which people deal with death or dying. Her studies and subsequent writings brought mainstream awareness to the sensitivity required for better treatment of individuals who are dealing with a fatal disease.

*Make no mistake,* ADDICTION IS A FATAL DISEASE. *If you don't get a handle on the disease, the disease will get a handle on you. There is a very real chance that an addict will not or cannot get sober, and there is always a very real chance that the addiction will end in the death of the addict. This is a sad reality, but one that must be considered and faced. The strong emotions that come from this reality have to somehow be digested, or processed. Otherwise, we become sick with worry, anxiety and stress, which all eventually manifest in a physical form of ill health or disease.*

These stages also apply to loss due to divorce or other emotionally traumatic experiences. Sometimes if you aren't already in the final stage of acceptance, it is difficult to move forward. However, hopefully, understanding will help you be open to the final stage so you can accelerate the process of regaining your life and your peace of mind, and moving forward toward healing.

The five stages are as follows:

1-Denial – Everything is fine. This kind of thing only happens to other people. This can't be happening to me. This is only temporary; it will pass.

2-Anger – Why me? This is not fair! Who can I blame for this?

3-Bargaining – If I can stop this, I promise I'll do better in the future. I promise to change. If only I had done things different.

4-Depression – What's the point in trying? I miss the person I used to know. Why is this happening to me, I'm not strong enough to handle this? If this person is not happy, I can never be happy.

5-Acceptance – I can't fix this, or I can't fight this. Everything will be okay. I may as well be ready for the outcome. I can make myself okay.

Everyone loses people they love, because we all have an expiration date. It is truly a tragedy when someone dies younger than we think they should, but if we're honest, death should never be unexpected. We all lose our loved ones and our loved ones all lose us at some point. When this happens you will more than likely experience this sequence of emotions. You really can't force the movement from one stage to the next. You must experience these as steps of a staircase, one leading to the next, and the next, and the next. So very often people get stuck in the depression stage; they either can't move on due to psychological issues, or they refuse to. They just get stuck in the pain and cling to it. These stages can happen as the result of other types of broken relationships, also, not just divorce or death.

**Denial** – This is typically a defense mechanism. As is with addiction, both the addict and the circle of concerned people ignore what is happening; usually in the beginning stages and sometimes longer. Simple denial is just as it sounds. You can simply deny the entire situation like nothing serious is happening, which makes it much less traumatic. You may also minimize the situation, another form of denial. No one takes the situation seriously enough in the denial stage and responsibility and accountability are passed over. For the most part, addicts will remain in the denial stage until they commit to some kind of recovery. Acknowledging denial or abandoning denial in the form of admitting, is the first step required in a 12 step program. Later as you pass through this part of your life, if you make the choice to move toward a more healing state, this stage of denial will have been an excellent learning experience. When death occurs, this stage is usually the stage of disbelief and shock.

**Anger** – You may experience changes in your body language, in your facial expressions, in your mannerisms, in aggressive behavior. You may experience negative effects to your health, to your relationships, and to your mental state. This stage is necessary to "stay safe." It is okay to be angry. It is okay to express your anger because it feels like someone has stolen pieces of your soul, and pieces of your life. It is okay to express anger that someone you love is destroying themselves. You may exhibit anger toward the addict, and you will most likely exhibit anger toward yourself. Often, anger will accelerate to rage. A key point we want to remember is the fact that *you cannot solve a problem on the same level it is created.* Too much anger or too much rage is toxic. You must find a way to control your anger. It is extremely likely that your anger will be directed toward someone else and you must manage it. Being angry is a natural process, but rage is undigested anger that hasn't been processed properly. With death or divorce, anger often occurs at the loss of the other party. Even though the anger in that case is due to heartbreak, it still needs to be managed and processed. Sometimes with death, the passing of time will take care of this step.

**Bargaining** – You are most likely more eager for the addictive situation surrounding you to change, than the addict is. Blackmail doesn't work, promises don't work, offering something in exchange for sobriety doesn't work. *The cost of bargaining often exceeds the gain. Bargaining or negotiating is always about value.* There is the creation of value, and the claim of value; rarely are the two equal. Someone gives, someone gets; someone loses, someone wins. When bargaining with an addict, you are negotiating with a person who is either *under the influence or seeking the influence,* or thinking about how they can use the negotiation to further their own agenda. I guarantee it, the addict will only heal, when, and if ever, the addict is ready. Unfortunately sometimes, children are involved as loved ones, and personal relationships are used in the bargaining process. Human beings are not to be bartered. Children are not a job, or collateral to be used as a bargaining tool, they are your family. Treat this sacred relationship as such and keep them safe, no matter what the cost. This bargaining stage is about dealing with grief or loss, thinking if we act a certain way or offer something up, we make ourselves feel better. However, none of that actually changes the situation. This is just an error in thinking due to grief.

**Depression** – So much can be said regarding this subject. Both the addict and you will experience these 2 stages: denial and depression. Many addicts who have decided upon a life of recovery are plagued by post-addictive depression. Many family members or personal relationship partners may experience extended bouts of depression, even if the addict is able to recover.

Depression is a complicated subject for which I am not qualified to speak. Have I experienced it? Yes, I have. I've also seen others experience it, but can only speak to my own experience about how I felt and how I moved on. It can be caused by the traumas that occur in our lives due to addiction, death and loss, but it can also be directly linked to meaning and purpose, and the lack thereof. Lives affected by addiction frequently suffer from lack of meaning and purpose, and when someone loses a loved one they feel like the meaning and purpose of their life is gone. Scientific studies have proven that those with some kind of spiritual assistance can deal more aggressively and more effectively with depression, than those with no spiritual connection. Depression is a result of being stuck in an emotionally traumatic situation and the inability to move on. There are situations where nothing particularly traumatic has happened, but a chemical imbalance in our bodies results in depression, and it can be numbing just as some drugs are. This is a result of an extreme Vata imbalance starting with worry and anxiety, leading to an extreme Kapha imbalance with characteristics of heaviness, sluggishness, sadness, a desire to sleep too much and overwhelming stagnation.

None of the five stages can be rushed and usually transition with no physical appearance, as they are all largely psychological. However, the physical manifestations of psychological pain can surely happen! Each is a healing and learning phase that leads to the next. If you are perpetually stuck in the depression stage, you are then very sick psychologically, and probably physically by now, and you need to care for yourself by seeking help. You can only heal in a healthy and appropriate manner by finally moving into the acceptance stage.

**Acceptance** – This is the final stage. You have to be able to accept the situation as it is, as it has been, and probably the most difficult acceptance of all, is to be able to accept things as they move into the future, no matter what! This is known as radical acceptance. We can only control ourselves, our situations, our emotions, our thoughts and our circumstances. We cannot control someone else, or change the circumstances they create. We can love them from a distance, but remain detached from the outcome of their addiction by changing the way we respond, and by changing our own experience. When someone is a Veteran who has seen the horrors of war, or when someone is a child who had destructive forces restrict their development during childhood, this step might never happen. This can be challenging when a parent loses a child, or if there have been other extremely traumatic events that act as a stop sign for our progress. Medication and therapy might be required for some people who are so affected they just can't move forward without help. This doesn't make someone weak, nor does it make them incapable; it makes them vulnerable and human. Never be ashamed to ask for help if you need it. Mental health assistance is better now than it ever has been, and you need to experience some relief through releasing whatever trauma you have experienced.

One powerful example of acceptance is the serenity prayer used in recovery meetings: *Grant me the serenity to accept the things I cannot change, the courage to change the things I can, and the wisdom to know the difference.* This affirmation or prayer verbalizes acceptance. Accepting means laying down of arms, being brave enough to simply stop the melodrama and walk away, and taking control of your own thoughts, hopes and dreams, and directing your own life. You have to practice a certain amount of detachment in order to accomplish this. Some addicts have to completely detach from their old life in order to create a new one. A small step of emotional and physical detachment sometimes needs to turn into relocation and cutting all ties with relationships and locations from the past. *Remember, suffering doesn't have to be a part of proving love.* It's important for your own health and well-being to step away from suffering. Detachment is a sign of strength and courage, not a sign of not caring or inconsideration. Detachment just means you are not emotionally pulled into what someone else is feeling or what someone else is experiencing. You have to be in control of your own feelings. Blaming someone else for how you feel is like trying to pull up your pants by pulling on the bottom of the legs first; it just doesn't make any sense. As an adult we have the ability to let go of our past and to make new choices about our life. Loving someone with compassion and empathy is loving someone without giving all of yourself away. You feel a lot of sincere remorse and concern for what they are going through, but you don't give up your own personal power to go through it with them.

The paradigm of addictive relationships includes 3 basic levels; I like to call them the 3 D's: Devastation, Destruction, and Dissolution. It doesn't matter if you love someone who is addicted or if it is the addict themselves, the relationship is still the same. All of the healing principles in this book will assist the healing process whether it is a relationship we have with someone else, or a relationship we have with ourselves.

With the acknowledgement or awareness of addiction comes devastation. Devastation is experienced as a wave of ruin and wreckage surrounding the addict. The friends, family and acquaintances, and even the addict themselves, are devastated by the addiction. Devastation includes disappointment from realizing the addiction, blaming and the "why me" stages. Devastation manifests as the emotional consequences of addiction.

Once the initial devastation is experienced, destruction settles in. This is the tangible, visible annihilation and obliteration of, well, pretty much everything; the physical body, the mental body and the spirit, and physical possessions as well as love. Here comes the destruction of employment and relationships, the destruction of physical and mental health, and the variety of other broken pieces of a life resulting from the destruction of an active addiction. Depression falls into this category, as well. As you push and shove along with the addict and focus all of your attention and emotion on them and their addiction, your own life suffers; your own soul suffers. The quality of your life suffers, and you misinterpret it as caring for them. Depression can lead to the destruction of your soul, and the destruction of your ability to lead a normal life. Some individuals remain in a perpetual state of destruction, doing nothing more than hoping that the situation will fix itself. Hope is important, as is faith, but it takes the power of intention and energy in the form of action to make any kind of real change.

Dissolution is the finality of acceptance. This manifests as detachment and the abolishment of relationships, either literally or a change in energy of the relationship. Dissolution resembles a "washing your hands of the situation," or "throwing in the towel," scenario; maybe even waving the white flag. At some point, you will tire of the drama and the games that are played. You will make the decision to dissolve the status quo of the relationship, and the dissolution, unfortunately, can sometimes occur due to the death of the addict.

The 3 D's represent a triangle with three sections. Dissolution or dissolving the current relationship is obviously the most important stage, and should always be at the base of the triangle. If devastation or depression are the strongest component of a relationship, the triangle is inverted and unstable. Dissolution of the dysfunction is the only way to strengthen the base that will maintain the relationship in the long term.

You must detach yourself from the addictive relationship in order to dissolve the relationship you currently have with the addict. Focusing all of your attention and energy on them, worrying countless hours, obsessing over their health and well being, only brings on more dysfunction and disease. By not dissolving the current relationship you have, you remain in a perpetual cycle of devastation and destruction, both of which lead to depression.

By dissolving the relationship, it does not mean to abolish all contact, or ignore, it means to dissolve *the current* relationship you have. *You need to take the steps to change the relationship you have with yourself, and then change the way you relate to the addict.* Distancing yourself from the addiction and setting your own boundaries, is in effect, dissolving the current relationship. Raising your vibration and increasing your own energy by learning and then applying, these steps for self-nurturing and care are just the boost you need to change everything. When you change your experience by changing the way you care for your whole self, you change your perception. This will only increase your compassion and empathy for others who are stuck in their suffering. It will increase your sense of understanding and allow you to sincerely care without being stuck in suffering with them.

**Dissolution is the
only stable base.**

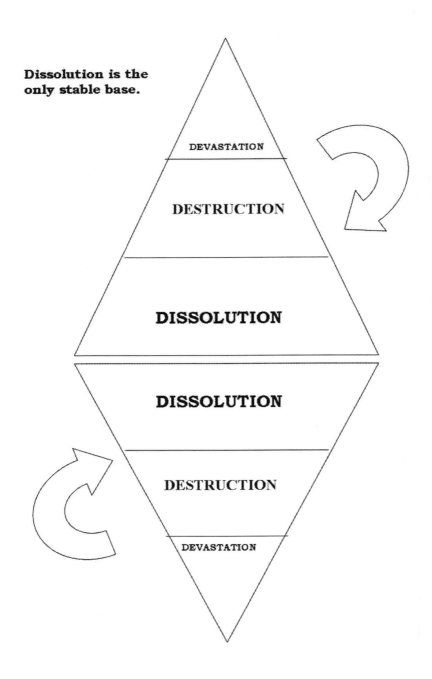

Disease is a body in a state of "dis" ease, or ill at ease. Establishing homeostasis, or returning the body to a state of ease, dissolves the devastation and destruction brought about by the stress and sickness that affects everyone in the perimeter of addiction.

Everyone has dysfunction and pain in their life in some form. The source of this can be identified with a fair amount of effort, but requires an enormous amount of honesty. Sometimes we are the ones standing in our own way. Once the source is addressed, take the steps to alleviate the suffering; put in place the intention and action of relief through release. Let go! You can't blame your suffering on someone else or they still have control over your life because you are allowing it. You can resolve the source of suffering in your own life, but not in someone else's. Nowhere else is this more apparent than with addiction. When and if the addict is ready to move on they will; either way, you must accept it. Watching a loved one destroy their life and themselves is never an easy task, but acceptance is one of the healthiest and highly championed feats you can accomplish.

Be careful not to confuse happiness with acceptance; it is a form of relief that can eventually lead to happiness, but the two don't necessarily go hand in hand. You may make a move to be happier, but when someone you love is suffering, happiness is complicated. Happiness is a choice. You can choose to be internally happy because of your own choices, and by choosing activities that make you happy. You can still feel sympathy and empathy for someone, while feeling joyful and happy on the inside. It's a lot like mental gymnastics, you have to learn it, you have to practice it, and you have to apply it.

No one jumps out of bed in the morning, if they have a bed, and exclaims to the world "Hey, I want to be a junkie!" More often than not, if you can get beyond even one layer of denial, you will find that the person you are dealing with wants to quit, wants to get help, wants to stop the crazy behavior. You must learn that the addict and the addiction are entirely separate. The addiction is something the person does, not the person themselves. I have rarely met a person who smokes that at some point hasn't expressed a desire to quit. Addiction is a jacket the person wears. Addicts so deeply identify themselves with their addiction they can't see the separation of the jacket from their own skin. When you deal with, or see the addict, see the person independent of the jacket they are wearing. Hopefully, for your sake, and for theirs, they will someday remove the jacket, hang it on a hook and free themselves. You can still care about the person wearing the jacket, but don't commit your mind to thinking they are an addiction, because they are not.

If you need help to get to a point where you can practice acceptance, even in part, seek a treatment program and counseling that you are comfortable with. Sometimes even just a support group with like minded people can help. Trained professionals can go where you cannot go; they understand how to reach the parts of an addict you cannot reach. *You cannot fix this by yourself,* and in fact, this cannot be fixed. It must be managed, but it cannot be managed until you are a confident, functioning piece of the puzzle. Again, this is why it is so important for you to love yourself first, you have to rebuild your confidence and strength in order to function. It was mentioned before, and I'll mention it again, it is not necessary to suffer in order to prove love! You can still be okay and love someone who is not.

Unfortunately, part of the strength you have to gain is being ready to accept the consequences of your choice. Don't feel guilty for saying no, don't feel guilty for not enabling. You need to say no, and you need to state your boundaries, for your own sanity and safety. Inherently, we know this and the addicted person knows this; if the family leads, the addict may be prompted to follow. The addict does not have to conform to your lifestyle, but they do need to exhibit respect for your personal and physical space. *Make your boundaries known, and make sure you maintain them; consistency is key.* Make them follow the rules of your space, or make them leave. This is not an easy task. It will not get easier with time, either. However, by asking for what you need, you will force them into making choices. They may make wrong choices, but then they are accountable for the choices they have made. This takes an incredible amount of courage, consistency and strength! You can do this!

In order to eat an egg, you must first cook the yolk. If you crack the egg and attempt to eat either the yolk or the white separately, the two will run together. Even hardening the yolk just a little bit, will strengthen the integrity of the yolk, and it will become distinct from the egg white. Each can be seen separately, even in color, and can then be separated. The inner core has its own strength, and the white becomes stronger, not allowing anything to penetrate the inner core. The longer you cook the egg, the stronger the shell, the white, and the core become. The egg, once cooked and peeled, will almost bounce when fully hard boiled, whereas trying to bounce a raw egg would not provide the same results. Strengthening yourself is like cooking the egg.

Without a tough inner core, your exterior is easily penetrated, and you'll leak all over. If your outside shell is cracked even a little bit, some of the layer of the white may ooze out a little, but the tough inner core, or yolk, remains strong and can stand on its own, if it's cooked long enough. Reinforcement and habitual positive action are so important to be able to continue to say no you may not invade my space, or for the addict, no I refuse to use again. The principles shared in this book are proven to help us build our inner core so we can stand on our own; even if someone has cracked our outer shell.

Communication skills when dealing with a person who is troubled, possibly mentally ill, addicted or challenged in some way, are of the utmost importance. Conversations take place that make no sense and usually end up in a tug of war or worse. It takes the right expression of words to explain your needs. Messages can easily be misconstrued by the recipient leading them to believe there is something wrong with them, they need to be fixed, or they're just simply not good enough. It's a painful process and it's hard to take words back once they're "out there." Complete retreat by both parties may happen, psychologically and physically, simply due to exhaustion or surrender. There is no purpose in allowing a conflict to fester and grow. Eventually it becomes the 800 pound gorilla in the corner of the room that no one wants to discuss. Attempting to use good communication skills at that point complicates the issue, because by then, everyone has forgotten what the real issue may be.

Conflict is inevitable, even in the most stable relationships. Learning good communication skills is very important in interpersonal relationships and managing conflict. As we grow as a person, we have the ability to communicate more effectively. Conflict increases as interdependence increases, so enabling actually just perpetuates the conflict; at some point you just have to let go of each other. Our closest relationships are often our most difficult and volatile. Sometimes we treat those we love the most, the worst. We don't feel it's necessary to be on our best behavior because we are so close, and we take for granted that the continuing health of our relationship is based completely on our ability to know the other person. Unfortunately, we never really know anyone else the way we think we do. We can't, because who they are is a collection of their experiences in life, and if you recall, we can't have the same experiences as anyone else.

This is why communication is such a key to dealing with your addict. *As mentioned earlier, the addict only occupies two states of mind, under the influence, and seeking the influence (withdrawal).* You can't use typical communication methods with someone who can't reason rationally. Your communication has to be direct, to the point, with conviction, meaningful, and short. Don't mince your words; use words they'll understand. Make sure they understand that you are setting a boundary for yourself, and that their behavior will not be allowed to continue in your personal space.

*Words are necessary.* They are necessary to seek and offer forgiveness; they are necessary to express our emotions; they are necessary for educating us, but mostly, they are necessary for expressing our needs. What they aren't necessary for is hurting another human being, but they are often used as ammunition just for that purpose! If you can't speak clearly due to emotion or whatever reason, write down what you want to say and read it back later. This is a good idea also, because it gives you a chance to prepare what you want to say exactly the way you want to say it. You can state your needs from beginning to end and won't have to reach for the right words, or get confused while you're talking.

There have been many, many times over the years I wanted to, and needed to, ask my son to leave my house. Every single time, my guilt would overwhelm me. I was terrified that if I asked him to leave I would never see him again. Maybe he would overdose, maybe he would get in a car accident, maybe he would just be angry and stay away. It still makes my gut wrench to think about, and especially to do it. The way I handled it eventually, was to sit him down when he was in the right state of mind and explain to him my needs. I explained to him that I needed to feel safe in my own home. I told him I needed to be healthy in order to continue to make a living and to care for the other people in my life. I also told him I needed to set an example for my grandkids, but mostly I needed to maintain my relationship with my higher power. I explained to him that if I was feeling unsafe, disrespected or exposing my grandchildren to risk, I might react in a way that wasn't congruent with my beliefs. He and I are very close and we have had many deeply spiritual talks. We both love to write poetry and we both are empathic. When I explained to him that my number one relationship might be jeopardized, he seemed to understand. I've only had to ask him to stay away or leave a number of times I can count on one hand. In spite of all the chaos and all the dysfunction, the person who wears addiction as a jacket, understood and heard me. I love him for that. When I have had to ask him to leave, he has left without argument. Even in a rattled state of mind he understands that I am acting out of love and not anger.

Journaling is one of the most powerful tools when it comes to getting to know ourselves and for "getting the ugly out!" Regular journaling gives you the opportunity to go back and review things, and to learn things about ourselves. When you're overwhelmed with emotion and you just start writing, everything can come out. When you're done, everything is out and now you have effectively processed some of it, just by stating it, and you can move on to the next thing. I guarantee by the time you have finished writing, you will be a little bit tired and feel a little bit of release. This is why therapy is so helpful, because when you are telling someone things and they don't interrupt you, you can finish putting your thoughts fueled by emotions out into the universe. Then you can go back and deal with the important stuff later. It also allows you the ability to calm down and see things from a different perspective.

Just by writing situations down, you can go back, read them, reflect on them, and vividly see what could have been different. Recall in a conscious state can also be a very powerful tool. Spending 10 minutes at night prior to falling asleep and recalling the events of the day, can also help you see in your mind's eye what you would have, or could have changed, or how you could have handled situations differently to create a more positive outcome. Both journaling and recall, help you calm down and relax a little, and right before bedtime is a particularly good time to practice both. It helps to relax you before you try to fall asleep, and it takes all that irritating stuff out of your brain so you can experience more peaceful sleep. I keep a journal next to my bed and write down my dreams, thoughts I might be having that are either negative or positive, or even things I want to get done. There aren't any rules because it's my journal. I don't have to worry about the spelling or the grammar or the writing because it doesn't matter. It is just a record of my thoughts and my emotions and it doesn't matter to anyone else. It's a lot like taking out the trash.

Don't live in the past, but learn to review the recent past in order to make changes in the future. Take the time to learn things about yourself and your situation. If you make small changes everyday pretty soon they add up to huge changes.

I know a person who is a recovering alcoholic. She is one of the most kind, giving, generous, loving, beautiful people I have ever had the privilege to meet. She is a quality caregiver, a wonderful mother and grandmother, and a fantastic friend, and will literally give you the shirt off her back if you need it. Even still, she goes through periods of self-loathing, self-doubt, and depression. She obsesses over her health and sometimes turns to food during periods of her sobriety to feed impulses. Even in recovery, and after having remained clean and sober for decades, and learning the things she has about herself and her addiction, she is still able to justify her addiction in some twisted mechanism of defense. She views it as not having been as bad as someone using drugs, or someone gambling. She was "just" an alcoholic after all, and not some "piece of junk crackhead;" a term I have heard her use.

Watching someone destroy their lives on meth or heroin, for example, is much more detrimental in her mind, than watching someone drink themselves to death. Why? Because drinking is much more socially acceptable than drugs and it's legal. It's allowed in public, at weddings, birthdays, family get-togethers, business meetings, wherever! Imagine if a roomful of corporate executives got together for a business meeting and at the 2pm break decided to all shoot up together, rather than go for a drink.. Wouldn't we be mortified? I am not saying that everyone who has had a drink is an alcoholic, just that if they are suffering from addiction, the repercussions of that drink are the same as they are to the heroin addict. It does seem more possible for an alcoholic to function in a job and at family events, than a street hustler hooked on heroin. Eventually, though, it all shows up the same.

*What you eat in private shows up in public, so to speak!*

I guarantee that the afternoon drink won't be the last drink of the day for the alcoholic. It is socially acceptable for that person to pick up that drink in a room full of people, and even encouraged most of the time, but at the end of the day that person suffers emotionally, spiritually and physically just as much as the street hustling heroin addict, or the teenage meth addict who is trading sex for drugs.

When we talk about resolution of addiction being accomplished by communication, compassion and love, it isn't in the context of sitting in front of the fire wrapped in a warm blanket sipping hot cocoa together, hugging it out. It is in the context of saying what you mean, and meaning what you say. It's about having compassion in your words, because of your new found understanding that the person you are communicating with is a sick individual. I'm talking about the altruistic kind of love; the kind of unconditional love shown to mankind by spiritual leaders.

You may have fallen into the communication void by now, where the only type of communication you have is filled with drama, screaming and yelling, filthy language and empty threats. Altruistic love is not only feeling and applying love toward the addict, but also toward you. You deserve it, you've earned it, and you're worth it; live your life the way you intend it to be; don't let the other person's illness take that from you because then everyone is ill.

It took me many, many years to really learn this lesson about communication. One of my many paths in life led me to train as a Divorce and Child Custody Mediator for a period of time. I spent many hours learning methods of communication during times of conflict. That was like a deluge of epiphanies all at the same time. While I was learning to help other people communicate through their conflicts, I was learning a whole lot about myself and how I had handled it in the past. That was quite a lesson!

*Sometimes our rose-colored glasses not only need to come off, they need to be smashed on the floor.*

One of the most important lessons I learned to avoid the pitfalls of a conversation going nowhere, or escalating, is to express your needs followed by a justification. The words you use need to be words that express needs, also, not words that express emotions or describe the situation. Examples:

+ Why can't you turn off the lights when you leave a room? or, I need the power bill to be lower so we have more money for other things; please turn off the lights when you leave a room.

+ I hate it when you call me in the middle of the night!

    I need to get decent sleep in order to function at work; please don't call me in the middle of the night.

+ I'm sick and tired of worrying about you all the time!

    I need to work on my own mental health; I have a lot of people who depend on me.

+ You need to stop using and get yourself together!

    I need you to stay away from me when you are high; it depletes my energy and I don't feel good.

+ Why can't you just stop what you're doing?

    I need to understand more about what you're going through, so I can try and help you find someone who can help you.

+ I don't want any of your friends or people you associate with around me!

    I need to feel safe. I have chosen to make my home (or person, or whatever you need to interject here) a safe place by choosing who can or can't be here.

+ I don't want to be around you anymore!

    I need to be alone. I have chosen to make some changes in my life and I have chosen to stay away from certain behaviors that compromise my goals for myself.

+ You never spend time with the kids!

  I need you to be a better parent; everything we do affects their progress and I need to be supported.

+ I'm so tired of all this!

  I need space for myself so I can rest and feel better. I have to take a break from all this so I can care for myself better.

+ You are sucking the life out of me!

  I need to ensure my own security; I am not meeting my own needs when I allow distractions all the time.

+ Why can't you pick up your clothes?

  I need to keep the house picked up so I have time for other important activities.

Whoever it is you are speaking to may not hear you, or understand you the way you need them to. But, if you have stated your needs, and expressed to them why your need is important, then you are done communicating. Being direct and accurate reduces the risk that you'll get dragged into a conversation where there are only hurtful questions with no answers. When you say what you mean and mean what you say, there is no more to say because you've already said it all! Especially when you add a justification behind it.

Stay away from adjectives that describe the negative traits of the illness of the person. They already know and it just becomes even more demoralizing and demeaning. It reinforces all of the disgust they already feel and it fuels their addiction with a "see I told you so" attitude. Also stay away from questions they can't answer. When we are in a negative emotional state we often throw questions out of desperation or confusion and it only causes both people involved in the conversation to be confused and desperate. Make your statements about you and your needs, and leave words like you or them out of the conversation. You shouldn't be telling them what they need, you should be telling them what you need and why.

When you say things like, "I love you, why can't you just stop," you're immediately putting conditions on the love you stated. It sounds more like "I love you, but I only love you if you don't act this way." This can be hard to get used to if you've been communicating the same way for a long time. When you say exactly what you need and why, don't feel like the silence or their inability to respond is awkward, because you haven't given them anything to work with and that's a good thing. You've made it about you without attacking them. You've stated your needs and told them why without addressing their needs, because you don't know what they need; only they know. This will automatically confuse them and sometimes that can be the end of the conversation.

Another extremely important concept in communication is gratitude. Even in the worst of circumstances, if you start a sentence with thank you, or thanks for that, or I appreciate it, or some acknowledgement of gratitude, it can be a game changer. Thank you for being patient with me, thank you for allowing me to tell my side of the story, thank you for.......whatever it is. You are setting the tone of the conversation and starting with something so positive it can't be rejected. Take care not to let this appear snarky or sarcastic, but feel it and mean it. Every single conflict and challenge in our life comes with a lesson, but we have to be willing to acknowledge it, learn it, and then apply it. Showing change through action is very powerful when you have decided to implement change in your life. Example is far more important than trying to explain to someone how you intend to change.

Relief through release of emotions through words is powerful. Whether you journal it or whether you speak it out loud it is expelling it from you. You can write it down and then burn it. You can scream it at the top of your lungs outside when you're alone and then throw rocks until you feel better. You can scream into a pillow and beat your fists on a mattress. Visualizing pushing your emotions out and disposing of them is just as powerful, if not more powerful, because when we use visualization it bypasses our intellect and goes directly to our subconscious. This is how hypnosis and neuro-linguistic programming also work. Our subconscious is put to work making changes while we continue to go about our business and before you know it, you start to become conscious of change happening.

I developed a presentation pertaining to one of the modalities of healing I learned over the years. I rented a venue and had a conference scheduled where at least 100 people were to show up. I had two friends there to help me take tickets and organize. One person showed up that day. It cost me quite a bit of money to organize the event, and I was stunned! I decided that I was going to go ahead and do my presentation in that great big room for that one person, just as I would if the room was full, so I did. After my presentation, she thanked me and began to tell her story and what had led her there that day. She had experienced every kind of abuse imaginable as a child. She had tried to tell people at her school, and her grandparents had been part of the abuse and she had a small family, no one whom she could trust. At the age of 10 she developed thyroid cancer. She had a large scar all across her throat. Due to all of the abuse and her inability to speak her truth, to express herself and to ask for help, her throat chakra was blocked. This energetic, vibrational chakra that regulates our speaking and our speech shut down, and manifested a physical disease. Shortly after that her 14 year old brother committed suicide; he was unable to endure any further abuse. During her teen years she developed addiction issues and in her early 20's she entered recovery. She was successful in recovery and now has four children of her own. Instead of becoming a victim, she made the choice to learn, heal, and develop her attachment to a higher power. She was what she deemed a "Gaia Grower." She now does readings and has her own business doing readings and acting as a healing practitioner. The lesson I learned that day was that the one person who was supposed to show up, showed up. It mattered to her to be there that day, and it mattered to me for her to be there. I still keep in contact with her once in a while and I can only hope she learned as much from me that day as I learned from her.

Deep breathing, or pranayama as it is known in the science of yoga, is a great way to calm down in the moment, reduce blood pressure and heart rate, calm our mind and get grounded. Most of us during the day practice shallow breathing. We breathe into our neck, shoulders and upper chest. When we focus on our breathing and breath deeply, we fill our lungs and into our lower abdomen, and it sends a signal through our body to calm down and be in a state of rest and relaxation. There are multiple health benefits to deep breathing and controlling the breath, including weight loss. There are many benefits to drawing in that extra oxygen. A great breathing exercise known as coherence breathing can be very helpful.

You can do this anywhere for just a couple of minutes a day. Sit comfortably and breathe in deeply to a 4, 5 or 6 count. Hold the breath for one or two counts, and then breath out to whatever count you chose, plus one. As an example, breathe in to a count of 5, breath out to a 6. If that seems too much, then breathe in to a count of 4, and breath out to a count of 5. This is a good exercise to do right when you wake up in the morning while you're sitting on the edge of your bed. It can be done anywhere and any time you can fit it into your schedule. If you suffer from anxiety, this is a very grounding exercise. If you have high blood pressure or other similar issues, this helps to reduce your blood pressure when you practice with focus.

We have a process in our nasal cycle where one side is more open for 3 hours or a little more, and then our biology automatically switches to the other side. This explains why when we have a stuffed up nose one side is more plugged than the other and then seems to switch. There is a breathing practice known as muladhara, or alternate nostril breathing. This exercise can open both sides of your nasal passage allowing more oxygen to your brain. Again, sit comfortably. Plug your right nostril with your right thumb. Take a deep breath in through your left nostril, then plug the left nostril with your right ring finger and breathe out your right nostril. Breathe in your right nostril, and then plug that nostril again with your right thumb. Breathe in the left nostril and out the left nostril, then plug with the right ring finger. Continue this alternating process until you feel like you are finished. Sit quietly for a moment and enjoy the benefit.

If you are a person who works on a computer frequently, get up and walk around at least once every hour. These breathing exercises are a good way to detach from the screen time for just a couple of minutes if you aren't able to get up and walk around. Breathing like this reduces stress and has a whole host of health benefits. After you finish your breathing exercises you can exercise your eyes.

Do each of the following moves with both eyes for 15 seconds each. This is a total of 2 minutes for a full workout for your eyes. It reduces stress and increases blood flow.

- look up to the left
- look up to the right
- look down to the left
- look down to the right
- look to the left
- look to the right
- look up
- look down
- roll your eyes around in a clockwise circle a couple of times
- roll your eyes around in a counterclockwise circle a couple times
- cup both hands and hold them over your eyes (this is called palming and is very soothing as the heat from your hands relaxes your eyes). If you work on a computer a lot, or read a kindle, palming can be very soothing to your eyes. Take a break every now and then and pay attention to your body!

We have a nerve in our bodies called the Vagus nerve. It is our body's largest nerve and runs from the brain, through our face, down our chest area and down to the abdomen. It regulates our respiratory rate, our heart rate, our digestion. It also regulates reflexive actions like vomiting, coughing, sneezing and swallowing. This nerve sends information from our internal organs to our brain. This nerve is the main contributor to our parasympathetic nervous system. Our sympathetic nervous system is our biological fight or flight response that helps us stay safe in threatening situations. However, being in that fight or flight response state sends our body stress signals, along with stress hormones. Our parasympathetic nervous system tells our brain when it's time to relax. We have the ability to activate this vagus nerve to make our body relax and bring us back to a parasympathetic state of calm..

When our sympathetic nervous system is engaged our blood vessels constrict, our blood pressure goes up, our heart rate goes up, our urinary and intestinal sphincters constrict and it reduces blood flow to the gut. We tense up, we are stressed out! This is important if we are preparing to fight or flee and need to save ourselves from some acute situation. However, this is not a state we want to stay in for the long term. It depletes our energy, it causes inflammation, it starves our organs from blood flow and it wears us out! When our parasympathetic nervous system is engaged our blood vessels dilate, our blood pressure goes down, our heart rate goes down, we have increased blood flow to the gut, we have increased saliva, and a relaxed state is an automatic benefit of all this.

Remember in a previous chapter we talked about our gut microbiome and how important it is to maintain a rich and diverse gut bacteria colony? We also learned that 70-80% of our immune system is in the lining of our gut. Well, guess what? The vagus nerve is an axis between our brain and our gut and is responsible for the connection of the cognitive and emotional areas of the brain with the intestinal functions of the gut. It is the super highway for boosting your immune system, making your organs happy, acting as an anti-inflammatory and telling your brain everything is going to be okay! It also acts as a food intake and satiety regulator. So how do we tickle our vagus nerve for maximum benefit? I hope you're ready for this long list of ways you can improve your health for free. Vagus nerve stimulation creates serotonin, among other things, and the medical community actually uses vagus nerve stimulation to treat depression, PTSD, inflammatory disorders, and other issues. This list pulls together everything we've learned so far. In order to experience real relief through release, activate your vagus nerve! Do yourself a huge favor and laugh your ass off!

+ Chanting mantras
+ yoga
+ meditation
+ singing, humming
+ massage
+ foot massage
+ eating fiber
+ gargling
+ exercise
+ deep breathing
+ LAUGHTER

# CHAPTER TEN:

## *Step Seven: Understanding Who We Really Are*

One of the most detrimental issues that lends to a chaotic environment is an untrained and untamed mind. Learning to control your thoughts and your actions requires controlling your mind and your responses. It's not the easiest thing you'll ever attempt, but it is one of the most productive. All day we have scenarios and conversations running through our mind that will never actually happen. We know with 100% certainty that we will have thought after thought after thought, but we don't really know what our next thought will be. A good share of our thoughts are negative, about how much there is to do, how depressed and angry we are over certain issues, how that person at work affected our performance negatively, and it just goes on and on! This unmonitored activity takes up a lot of energy and is directly responsible for a lot of fatigue and depression. Endless, repetitive thoughts can be the ruin of us!

Our mind, which took millions of years of evolution, suddenly becomes a nuisance when we give into our rapid thought stream.

However, we do not have to attach to our thoughts and buy into them. We can simply become aware of them and then let them roll on by. Don't believe everything you think!

One of the major teachings of a 12 step program is the belief in a higher power. The statistical rate for continued sobriety is astronomically higher for those who have a belief system; this holds true for all people. There is now a wealth of information, and easy access to information, that proves that energy outside of our self is affected by us, and we are affected by it. Everything is an exchange of energy and information and therein lies the solution to everything. Change the energy and change the information (or change the input and change the output).

If you already have a belief in a higher power, then relying on that belief system, or having faith, is not too difficult because you have a foundation. If you recall in an earlier chapter we learned it doesn't matter what kind of higher power you put your faith into. If you have faith in what you see, hear, smell, taste, and touch, then you have faith in your five senses. If you have faith in statistics, numbers and studies, then you have faith in science. If you have faith in a spiritual entity or realm, or religious dogma, then you have faith in the philosophy and writings of that.

The higher power of the mind and its relationship to the energy around us is actually the power of our own consciousness. As our awareness grows we seem to experience a greater level of consciousness, but it has always been there, we just operate on autopilot and tend to ignore. We are connected to the source of all things as a collective consciousness. It is only when we start to seek to become whole again, we begin to pay attention to synchronicities, and we seek a reconnection to our eternal self, which is our pure consciousness.

The higher power that you need to give you the strength to make your life right, and to move to a higher level of living, is already within you, and surrounds you; it believes in you so it doesn't matter if you believe in it. All of the principles shared in this book are about letting go, getting rid of, releasing, detoxifying and shedding; not about adding more. In order for real change to happen we have to detoxify our body by eating better food and allowing our biology to work at an optimum level. In order for us to detoxify our mind, we have to stop sending negative sensory impressions. We do this by making different choices to create positive sensory impressions by using our five senses to balance in the ways we learned in previous chapters. We also need to detoxify our emotions. Before this can happen, we have to be able to uplift our biology and our mind, so that we can calm down again and allow ourselves the ability to respond instead of react. We have to understand that we only have negative emotions, which cause negative physical feelings, or we have positive emotions, which cause positive physical feelings. Internally, our physiology responds to what we are telling ourselves. If we tell ourselves we are happy, then our body becomes happy; if we tell ourselves we are sad, then our body becomes sad. The same goes for eating and sensory impressions. Touch, taste, smell, see and hear good things, and all the rest falls into place.

The only "thing" you need to activate change has always been there, inside of you, and it gets stronger as we create better experiences and learn throughout our lives. There is no need to look outside of yourself for answers or for healing. It gets stronger as we practice our daily routines and implement mindfulness in our life. It gets stronger as we eat right for our essential nature and begin to heal our biology. It gets stronger as it activates our own healing impulses through sight, sound, smell, taste and touch. It gets stronger as we activate our body systems through exercise and mindful movement. It gets stronger through releasing toxic emotions, letting go of blame, and the traumas we relive on a daily basis.

If we are going to interact with the behavior of addiction on the same level as the addiction, then we need to work the 12 steps of A.A., also. The only way an issue can be solved is on a higher level and that is why it is so important to seek a higher power. Let that higher level be our pure consciousness, mindfulness, spirituality and an altruistic love for another human being; with no judgment. Again, suffering is not a part of proving love and you can't fix somebody else or create their experience for them. Stay in your lane and focus on yourself and let the story play out while you just do the right thing. Yes, it can be painful and agonizing, but once we've experienced a higher level we can never go back. When we falter, we always have something to reach up for to pull us back to higher ground.

A study conducted by Stanford University researchers showed how we aren't just passive observers just perceiving reality as it is, but that our minds actually change reality. They found that a person's mindset actually affects their health. Mindset has everything to do with reducing anxiety, lowering blood pressure, easing pain and boosting immune systems, and everything in between. The study also showed that those that expect pain, ruminate on pain, feel helpless about pain, and get even worse pain. This is particularly true when it is chronic pain. This is being studied further to try to reduce opioid use. Those who use opioids to reduce pain are afraid to stop taking them, thinking it will worsen their pain. Instead of changing their mindset or looking for other healing options, they rely on the surety of the pill and live in a state of fear. Another positive result of the study showed that people with a fixed mindset of growth believed more in their own abilities of talent and intellect. We don't have to accept things the way they are because they are always changing and our perception is so limited, that what we think we see is only minutiae in comparison to what really is.

There are well over a thousand studies conducted on meditation. Meditation is not something we do, it is something we experience. I like to say prayer is asking and meditation is receiving. It is a tool we use to calm the mind and to step away from our racing thoughts for a bit. We do exercise to work out our bodies to stay in shape and improve performance. We study, learn things and analyze things, or do games and puzzles to work out our brain to keep it in shape and improve performance. Some people attend church, attend ceremonies and perform rituals, or spend time in nature to improve their spiritual performance. Meditation is what we use to tone and improve the performance of our mind.

Meditation is the practice of calming the mind, becoming aware of the multitude of thoughts that invade the empty spaces of the mind, but not becoming attached to those thoughts. It is a practice in detachment and healing. So many qualified medical studies support the psychological, physiological, biological, emotional and spiritual healing benefits of meditation, it is being used to treat a multitude of diseases and disorders. In places all over the world there are statues in areas where meditation takes place. The statutes will have certain hand positions, and these are intentional. Hand positions indicate grounding, receiving, or gratitude, for example. Before starting any meditation it is important to set an intention. The intention can be anything you want it to be, and it's likely your intentions will change from day to day based on what you need in your life at that moment. Your intention will be something to do with grounding, receiving or gratitude, so you are free to use hand symbols when you meditate, also. It helps our psychology when we support our activity with symbols or items that we believe hold power. Healing ourselves or someone else is always a good intention before starting a meditation.

Before someone can sit in meditation, they have to at least have the ability to sit still if even for a few minutes. Some people do not have that ability if they are affected or afflicted, so all of these other steps we have explored are a way to calm the body and the emotions before you calm the mind, so that you can experience meditation. There are a lot of different ways to meditate so you have to find something that works for you. The best time to meditate is first thing in the morning, and again mid-afternoon. Morning meditation is important because you haven't had any distraction thrown your way yet, and you are still in a relaxed state of mind. The mid-afternoon meditation is important because it puts you in a relaxed state before you deal with evening things and prepare to rest for the night. It's not a good idea to meditate just before bed because you will likely fall asleep.

Everyone has a different schedule so you might only be able to meditate for 2 minutes. It is suggested that twice a day for 30 minutes is a good goal. Some people meditate for hours, and others may be able to accomplish what they need in 15 minutes. There are no rules and there is no right or wrong. It is you nurturing yourself, and you changing your experience, so what works for you, works for you. Very often when someone starts meditation they will fall asleep. This is okay. All that means is that you might be tired. Keep at it and eventually what you strive for will happen. It will happen. The only important thing is that you make yourself comfortable and try to avoid any distractions. It's a good idea to find a place where there aren't pets, kids, electronics, or other noise or distractions. As a support system, you can create a sacred space on a shelf, in a corner, in an entire room, or maybe your entire house or apartment. Everyone also has different living arrangements, so depending upon where you are and how you live, do what makes you comfortable. People are mobile, so of course you are not always going to be in the same space on a constant basis. However, setting up a place that holds power for you is important because it is part of the neuro associative conditioning we learned in a previous chapter. Having your space ready reminds you to meditate.

When a ceremony or ritual is performed in the same place or space on a continuous basis, and items are used, and meditation or prayer are performed, it creates a feedback loop. The ceremony or ritual becomes stronger, the items become stronger, and the meditation and prayer becomes stronger. The way this works is through energetics; each energizes the other and the power of the energy increases; it is a circle of energy. This is apparent in churches or in indigenous landmarks, or through practices like Feng Shui or Vastu; it is why there are certain places on earth that appear to exude or hold more energy in the form of power. This is known as conditioning. A study showed that when scientific experiments are conducted in a place or space where meditation is being performed, it changes the results of the experiment. The same experiment is performed, but the outcome is different because of the energy change in the space due to the meditation. A similar study was done with water; just by placing an intention and then meditating upon that intention and the water, the molecular structure of water changes. What it boils down to is quantum mechanics. We are part of all that is, and all that is, is part of us. If we can strive to use that for our own development, we operate much more efficiently and at a higher vibrational frequency.

Just as neuro associative conditioning trains our mind and assists us in associating healing processes with our five senses, meditation becomes a conditioning system for tangible things, our body, our mind and our environment; immediate and extended. It is also apparent in energy healing techniques. In Native America health and well being are intrinsically linked to spirituality. There is no separation between the land, the sky, the universe, the animals nor the person. It is all one energy, all one source of being.

The benefits of meditation happen immediately. Once you begin the process of stepping away from your thoughts. Just some of the health benefits include:

+ lower blood pressure
+ lower heart rate
+ reduced anxiety

+ reduced stress
+ reduced chronic pain
+ slower breathing
+ a reduction in metabolism

Meditation puts us in that parasympathetic state where we are at ease and relaxed, and it activates our vagus nerve, sending signals to our body that everything is okay.

One of the most fascinating benefits of meditation are the anti-aging effects. Telomeres are DNA and protein complexes that are located at the end of linear chromosomes and are necessary for the complete replication of DNA, as well as chromosome stability. They are kind of like the caps on the end of a shoelace. They shrink as we age and when they've shrunk, well, we're gone.

Interestingly, from a psychological perspective, telomere shortening can be accelerated by several behavioral factors, including poor diet, poor sleep, cigarette smoking, excessive alcohol consumption, drugs, sedentary lifestyle, and several psychological factors, such as personality characteristics, psychiatric disorders and psychological distress. Meditators show significantly better results in the measurements that were related to mindfulness abilities, such as attention and awareness, observing, describing, non-judging, resilience, self-compassion, and satisfaction with life and subjective happiness. Moreover, the expert meditators reported significantly lower experiential avoidance, anxiety, and depression. *AND, meditation is shown to decrease the shortening of telomeres, therefore increasing life span and overall health.*

Meditation is truly the key to the kingdom. It spontaneously begins the physical healing process, our mental healing process and is a doorway to developing a relationship with our higher power. There are many different methods of meditation. You just have to find one that works for you and stick with it. Learning about healing isn't enough; you have to apply the methods to create a new experience in your life. Once you have experienced something different, then you don't just have knowledge about it from studying it, you have experienced it and have a sense of knowing. This is akin to wisdom and the development of our cognition as we get older. It's impossible to know something on a deeper level just because you've learned about it; you must experience it to really understand it.

Here are some examples of different types of meditation and meditative practices:

- walking or being in nature
- staring into a flame (candle or fire)
- chanting or listening to chants
- drumming or listening to drums
- somatic dancing
- listening to music
- listening to binaural beats
- listening to guided visualization
- listening to guided meditation
- listening to singing bowls
- singing
- mala beads
- rosary beads

- recitation
- tai chi
- Qigong
- Yoga
- Sun gazing
- Staring at geometric or other visual patterns
- Trance states, Indigenous and Shamanistic traditions
- Contemplative prayer
- Primordial Sound Meditation
- ZaZen Meditation
- Transcendental Meditation
- Mantra Meditations
- Cabalistic practices
- Chakra focusing
- Deep, focused breathing, pranayama

If you have anxiety disorders, or have a hard time calming your mind, guided meditations are highly recommended. As you begin to experience change, you may get to a point where you can practice silent meditations. Guided meditations bypass your conscious mind and pass through straight to your subconscious mind. They are almost story-like and you don't have to work at ignoring or taming your thoughts because the storyline is moving you along with it. These are just as healing and just as relaxing. The practice of just quieting your mind and getting in touch with the deepest part of yourself is the goal, so however you do it, you are benefitting.

Focusing on each of the five senses, one at a time, is a simple meditation that can be used to engage with energy pretty much anywhere, anytime. Silently name one thing you can see, then one thing you can smell, one thing you can hear, one thing you can taste, and one thing you can feel. Repeat this, but name two things for each of your senses. You can go on to do three or four, and then to make it more energetic you can apply emotion to each one. You can do this while you're walking, sitting, or standing and it works with your eyes open, also. Energy flows where attention goes.

The intention of meditation no matter how you proceed, is to help you step away from your thoughts and create a state of calm and peace. It is also to reduce stress and improve your emotional well-being. It is a bio-psycho-socio-spiritual approach to health. In addition, it is the connection to all that is, to the source of all creation. You might get frustrated at first, or bored, or tired or experience other sensations, but if you stick with it, eventually you will have profound experiences. You must approach it with a sense of non-judgment and be gentle and kind to yourself.

Scientists can't even explain what consciousness "is," but meditation is a way we can begin to experience consciousness and become aware. Our brain operates at different frequencies known as Beta, Alpha, Theta and Delta. Beta is our state of normal activity where we are thinking, listening, talking and going about our business. Alpha is a little slower than Beta, and is an alert, but relaxed state. It kind of acts as a bridge between the subconscious and the conscious. Theta is a state that resides between deep sleep and being awake; where we are very relaxed. Delta is deep sleep with little movement or activity.

Theta frequency is a slow activity state. It is the state that connects us to daydreaming, meditation, and fantasy. It is the state where emotions, sensations and memories are stored. The frequency waves of Theta get stronger, not the activity, just the intensity of the waves, during meditation, prayer, and spiritual awareness. This is why these activities have such a profound effect on us. It reflects the state between sleep and being awake connects us to our subconscious mind. This state is not a normal state for adults to operate in, but is often normal for children up to the age of about 13 years. This is why children have the ability to just be in the flow and focus on their play. There is so much joy in watching a child create or pretend. This same joy can be relearned as an adult through the act of meditation. When you are able to train yourself to be in this Theta frequency long enough, the connection to the subconscious is almost unavoidable.

This is why you are almost guaranteed to have some kind of profound experience if you consistently practice meditation. The physical health benefits are motivation enough because the benefits are immediate. But if there is only one thing you can change in your life, let it be meditation. It is free, it can be done anywhere, anytime. It doesn't take any special skills or expensive learning. This connection to the unknown, to the silence and to the empty space between thoughts is who we are; who we really are. And, when we find out who we really are, everything about our life and our perception of life changes. This is an area where we can learn things we once thought were impossible to learn. It is an area where we can retrieve and process memories we didn't think we could recall. This is the space where we renew our biology, rejuvenate our mind, and connect with our spirit.

This space, or area, or place is not outside of us; it is us. It is a glimpse into our higher self and once seen, it cannot be unseen. It isn't something we can examine as separate from ourselves because it is effectively us witnessing our own process of inner transformation.

The study of the body's Endocannabinoid System is relatively new. It is a regulatory system for many of our body's physiological and cognitive processes. One study suggested that loss of the communication that can occur in this system might affect mood disorders and lead to drug abuse, and impact neurodegenerative neurodevelopmental disorders. These include disorders like anxiety, depression and psychosis; also, Alzheimer's, Parkinson's, and Huntington's. New information is always being discovered and studied and that gives us hope for the future.

Meditation is one of the things the studies showed to have an important effect on this endogenous cannabinoid system. Just think of the healing possibilities of that! What if we can just heal and prevent diseases and disorders through the power of intention and of realigning our body's own regulatory system?! That gives us hope.

# CHAPTER ELEVEN:

## *Conclusion*

While my son was incarcerated most recently, he passed out in the bathroom. He hit his head on the way down and blacked his eye and his chin; he also urinated on himself. He woke up, stood up and started to walk toward the common area and passed out again. He woke up to a guard slapping his face and asking if he was okay. He has degenerative disc disease and hurt his back and his shoulder on the second fall. His blood pressure was 89/89 and his pulse rate was over 120. When he relayed this to me, I asked if he had seen a doctor. He had not been given any kind of follow up medical care; not even to check his blood pressure. When you are a mother, it doesn't matter what age your child is or under what circumstances, when they are sick or in crisis and you can't get to them, it becomes a special kind of agony. The only tools I have to digest, respond to, and deal with these kinds of distresses I have experienced, are detachment and the healing principles I have learned. They are free and they are effective, and they are profound.

The only thing we know for certain in this life is the past. That's because our past is just an accumulation of our life experiences and our memories. We don't have much control over our experiences as children and sometimes even into our teen years. However, as adults we can make the choice moment by moment to create new experiences; better experiences and more healthy experiences. When we do this, we begin to revise our past because every second that passes becomes the past. We also change the unknown future because we are changing how we treat ourselves in the present moment. Choosing to create better experiences for ourselves is the catalyst for future change; real change, physically, emotionally and spiritually. When we change, the conditions around us change, then our environment changes, and that can change everything.

Attaching ourselves to the past, or to people or to material items, is done from a sense of fear and insecurity. We feel like if we attach ourselves we have some sort of control over the outcome of a situation, or the perpetual life of people and things. Money and creature comforts are wonderful things to have in this life; we need money to support our basic needs, but having enough is better than having too much or too little. Having enough creates a comfort zone and a certain balance in our lives. Money, things and people are all transient in our life, not by intention, but because that is just the nature of our existence.

I am a great believer in surrounding yourself with things that bring you joy and that invoke profound connections and emotions. This includes people and material items, music and even animals. This is one powerful way to balance ourselves through our five senses. But when we attach our identity or our happiness to these things, then our identity and our happiness is directly connected to their existence. Because they are transient, when they move on for whatever reason, if we have attached ourselves, we suffer emotional pain or a sense of discomfort from the loss.

The more money you have and the more things you have, the greater your fear becomes of losing it all. Too much "stuff" can create a sense of heaviness and being overwhelmed. Money gets moved to several different accounts and channels in an effort to hang on to it, things get stored, gates get put up, locks get put on things. A fortress begins to sprout up around us in order to keep our things, our money and our people to ourselves. Lots of people with a lot of money, probably most, are great philanthropists and they pump their wealth back into places and programs that make a real difference in the world. If that person just moves that money but doesn't vest themselves in the spirit of giving, or take part in the charitable activity, even if only emotionally by putting their heart into it, then there remains that void within themselves. They end up doing a lot of good in the world, but doing no good for themselves. True happiness is not at all about accumulation, it is about letting go, releasing, decluttering and detachment. It is also about creating the emotions within ourselves that instigate biological changes that cause healing effects.

Detachment is not relinquishing your dreams and desires. Likewise, it is not relinquishing your love for another human being, or even giving up your "stuff." Detachment is very simply having your intention and then focusing your attention on your activity and not the end result, or the outcome. Leaving room for flexibility in our life is a must; if we are too rigid in attaching ourselves to the final result, we can never be happy. As we accumulate education, wealth, material items, relationships and all other things in our life, if we hold steadfast to the finalization of these things, we will always be disappointed. These things are only new for a moment and the newness wears off, so we start to seek more and add more. Each time we make a different decision to seek or add something else, the final outcome changes, so we're really only attaching ourselves to something fleeting. It's much easier to admit that we don't have total and full control over things and circumstances in our lives. The only real finish line in our life is death; that's a given. We can strive for certain achievements and accomplishments and just learn to simply enjoy the journey on the way. We can also allow ourselves the kindness and nurturing that gives us the tools to be able to switch gears if things don't turn out our way.

Detachment from relationships can be especially important when you care for someone who is addicted. Undoubtedly, in this case, when you are rigidly attached to the outcome you can be repeatedly disappointed. The kind of disappointment suffered in this case can lead to serious physical health issues, which then lead to emotional and mental issues, making us as sick as the afflicted person. Detaching in this manner does not equal not loving. It does not equal not caring, or turning your back on someone. What it does equal is you putting you and your needs first, and not riding in the passenger seat of their illness while they drive. They can drive you right over a cliff if you allow it.

Addiction is a holistic disease. There is no part of the person that is not affected. You cannot separate the physical from the mental from the emotional torment that makes up the disease.

This can be why it is so incredibly difficult to treat. This is also why there is no answer for "why can't you just quit," or "why did you do that again," or any number of other questions. Addiction has so many little moments of victory along with so many little moments of defeat, sometimes in the same day or even hour, that it is maddening. It is maddening to the individual wearing the jacket of addiction and maddening to all those observing from the outside. It becomes very important to detach from the outcome of this relationship because between you and them, there is a disease creating barriers so large, sometimes they cannot be overcome.

When you detach yourself from a relationship, you still love that person very much and you empathize with their pain and suffering. You continue to wish them well and hope for the best and celebrate their victories, but you have to do the same for yourself. And, you have to do the same for yourself first. The only relationship you don't have to detach yourself from is your relationship with your higher power. That relationship becomes pure and empowering, and provides you the strength and wisdom to carry on no matter what, and it brings you to a new level of understanding.

Even the relationship you create with yourself will have outcomes that aren't expected, so we need to remain flexible in that relationship, too. We need to set our intentions and focus our attention on the activity of the relationship with ourselves. We do this by creating daily routines to provide stability, by eating right to nourish and strengthen our body, by exercising the right way for our unique nature, and by grounding ourselves and our emotions by balancing our senses and practicing meditative techniques. The physical, mental and emotional benefits happen automatically, and so does the increase in our conscious awareness. All we have to do is perform the action and apply a little mindfulness to it.

When someone attends a University they are bound by the rules of that University. When they have finished their studies and achieved their degree, they leave the University and they are no longer bound by the rules. This is the same with our personal growth and development. As we seek and achieve higher levels of thought and action, it leads us to seek and achieve higher levels of consciousness and being. This leads us to understand how responding on a higher level to people and situations in our life, instead of just reacting in the moment, can change our entire relationship environment. We start to understand we are no longer bound by the rules of common relationships, but by the universal rules of a deeper, more altruistic relationship, first with our higher power, then with ourselves, then with everyone else.

The first step toward real change starts with you. Once you take action to put in place these principles of healing, your life circumstances change through the process of autonomy. Those rules of self-government include better health, more stable emotions, less anxiety and worry, and ultimately enlightenment. At the center of our being there is bliss. We can carry this bliss with us everywhere and at all times, even while we grieve and even while we might feel physical pain. This becomes our torch that we carry to and pass on to, all of those we come in contact with. Our love and concern only grow deeper with increased compassion and greater empathy for the human condition, but most importantly for ourselves. Self love is one of the highest forms of love, and this love includes forgiveness and kindness, and then the courage to move on. This is true for someone who is addicted and for someone who cares about an addict. The only way to love an addict, is to love yourself first; even if you are the person wearing the jacket of addiction. If it is you, then take off that jacket and hand it to the people you love, and learn to love yourself first. They'll be happy to hang it up for you, and happy to see you happy.

I don't know how my story will end, but this is not my only story. I also have stories of joy, accomplishment, happiness, and other stories of sorrow. It's a life of jambalaya that I lead. I want the best for all of my loved ones, and more than anything else, I want all the things for them that are free. Fond memories of me, happiness, healthy relationships, and not too much, but just enough of whatever it is they desire in life. I think having just enough is better than having too much or too little. The only thing I know about my story is that if I'm honest, these fundamental truths I have shared here, saved my life before it was too late. Many, many times I have wanted to give up but a sense of real purpose kept me going. At first my purpose was to save my son, but as I learned, my purpose was to save myself and then help a multitude of others save themselves through the lessons I never wanted to learn.

# DOSHA QUIZ

Circle the number for the answer that is most like you. Some answers will be exactly like you and some will be similar or not at all like you. These are general questions, so just choose the answer that fits you the best. Answer the questions according to how you feel when you are at your best. This will tell you your essential nature, or dosha. Each of the 1. Answers relate to Vata. Each of the 2. Answers relate to Pitta. Each of the 3. Answers relate to Kapha. Total your scores at the bottom of the quiz. The dosha with the highest number is your dosha, and the second highest number is your sub-dosha. Don't add the numbers together, just tally up the total count for each number. There are a total of 18 questions, so the total number of your three scores should equal 18. EXAMPLE: 10 PITTA (#2) answers, 5 VATA (#1) answers, and 3 KAPHA (#3) answers would equal 18.

1. I'm normally slender and it's difficult for me to gain weight
2. I'm of medium build and can gain or lose weight easily depending on my diet and exercise.
3. I'm big boned and built heavier. I gain weight easily and it's difficult for me to lose.

1. I have dry eyes and they tend to flutter.
2. My eyes are somewhat sensitive to light and get red and sore easily.
3. I have nice, rounder eyes and they're normally clear.

1. My facial features tend to be slender, sharp and smaller.
2. My facial features tend to be heart shaped, and average in size.
3. My facial features tend to be round, smooth.

1. My skin is normally dry, thin, with protruding or obvious veins
2. I have sensitive skin that sometimes sunburns easily. Sometimes I have pimples, acne scars or moles, and my skin can tend to get reddish.
3. My skin looks smooth, moist, youthful. I tan easily, and my skin is clear.

1. My hair is dry and brittle and tends to fall out easily.
2. I have straight hair; it's not thin but not thick.
3. My hair is abundant and smooth.

1. My nails tend to be dry and brittle.
2. My nails tend to be smooth, pinkish and flexible
3. My nails are strong, thick and smooth

1. I have trouble falling asleep. I wake up often in the night and my sleep gets disturbed easily.
2. I am a moderately sound sleeper and wake up with a lot of energy.
3. I feel like I need a minimum of 8 hours of sleep, I sleep deep and I wake up slowly in the morning.

1. My hands and feet tend to be cold and I prefer warm weather
2. I feel warm most of the time and I prefer cooler weather
3. My body is cool but adapts to most weather. I prefer moderate weather

1. I hardly ever sweat
2. I sweat even when doing minimum activity
3. I sweat very little when doing moderate activity

1. I feel full even when I eat small meals. Sometimes I forget to eat and have irregular meal times.
2. I have a strong appetite and feel hungry frequently
3. I have a modest appetite and can skip meals easily

1. I have irregular digestion. I frequently experience gas, bloating or gurgling sounds in my gut after even a moderate meal
2. My digestion is quick and easy even after moderate meals
3. My digestion is slow. I feel lethargic and sleepy after moderately heavy meals.

1. When I'm stressed, I tend to suffer from anxiety and worry
2. When I'm stressed, I get angry and irritable
3. When I'm stressed, I tend to withdraw but remain calm

1. I am quick and spontaneous
2. I am organized and focused
3. I move and react slowly

1. I tend to speak very quickly and sometimes have scattered speech
2. I am direct, precise and clear in my speech
3. I am slow and monotonous in my speech

1. I have a good short term memory, but tend to easily forget
2. I have a good moderate memory
3. I have a good long term memory; once I grasp something, I never forget

1. I am very creative and can multitask, but sometimes I don't finish my projects
2. I prefer to have a plan in place and strive for perfection. I like to lead my own projects.
3. I am slow but dependable and steady. I usually don't multitask, but I always complete my projects.

1. I tend to get easily distracted
2. I'm focused if the topic is interesting
3. It's very hard for me to get distracted when I'm concentrating on something

1. I often feel fearful, anxious or uncertain; too many choices confuse me
2. I am ambitious, but can get irritated when my plans get interrupted
3. I am calm, and I love peace and quiet. I find solace in solitude

Total 1. (VATA) = _____

Total 2. (PITTA) = _____

Total 3. (KAPHA) _____

TOTAL SCORE = 18

# KAPHA:

This list is not all inclusive. Only eat when you are hungry, eat your last meal at least 3 hours before going to bed, reduce sweet, sour and salty foods, focus on bitter, astringent and pungent foods, use oils sparingly, foods should be light, airy, warm and dry

| FRUITS | VEGETABLES | VEGETABLES cont. |
|---|---|---|
| Generally most astringent or dry fruits | In General Most Pungent & Bitter Vegetables | In General Most Pungent & Bitter Vegetables |
| Apples | Artichoke | Onions |
| Applesauce | Asparagus | Parsley |
| Apricots | Beet Greens | Peas |
| Berries | Beets | Peppers, Sweat & Hot |
| Cherries | Bitter Melon | Prickly Pears |
| Cranberries | Broccoli | Radishes |
| Figs (Dry) | Brussels Sprouts | Rutabaga |
| Grapes | Cabbage | Spaghetti |
| Guava | Carrots | Squash |
| Jackfruit* (seasonal) | Cauliflower | Spinach Sprouts |
| Lemons | Celery | Squash(summer) |
| Limes | Cilantro (Coriander) | Tomatoes (yellowish and cooked) |
| Longan* (seasonal) | Corn | Turnip Greens |
| Lychees | Daikon Radish | Turnips |
| Peaches | Dandelion Greens | Watercress |
| Pears | Eggplant | Wheatgrass Sprouts |
| Persimmons | Fennel (anise) | **DAIRY** |
| Pomegranates | Garlic | No Dairy except Ghee and Goat milk |
| Prunes | Green Beans | Buttermilk |
| Raisins | | |

| | | Cottage Cheese (Skimmed Or Goats |
|---|---|---|
| Rambutan* (seasonal) | Green Chillies | |
| Strawberries* | Horseradish | Milk) |
| | Jerusalem Artichoke | Ghee* |
| | Kale | Goats Cheese (unsalted & Not Aged)* |
| | Kohlrabi | Goats Milk, Skim |
| | Leafy Greens | Yogurt (Goat milk) |
| | Leeks | |
| | Lettuce | |
| | Mushrooms | |
| | Mustard Greens | |
| | Okra | |
| **GRAINS** | **ANIMAL FOOD** | **\*All Spices Are Good** |
| Avoid wheat and rice (except basmati) | Chicken (White) | Ajwan |
| Amaranth* | Eggs | Allspice |
| Barley | Fish (Freshwater) | Almond Extract |
| Buckwheat | Rabbit | Anise |
| Cereal (cold, Dry Or Puffed) | Shrimps | Asafoetida |
| Corn | Turkey (White) | Basil |
| Couscous | Venison | Bay Leaf |
| Crackers | **NUTS** | Black Pepper |
| Durham Flour | Avoid nuts | Caraway |
| Granola | Charole | Cardamom |
| Millet | **SEEDS** | Cayenne |
| Muesli | Chia | Cloves |
| Oat Bran | Flax* | Cinnamon |
| Oats (dry) | Popcorn (no Salt Or Butter) | Coriander |

| | | |
|---|---|---|
| Polenta | Pumpkin | Cumin |
| Quinoa | Sunflower | Curry Leaves |
| Rice (Basmathi, Wild) | **SWEETENERS** | Dill |
| Rye | Fruit Juice Concentrates* (esp. apple and | Fennel |
| Sago | pear) | Fenugreek |
| Seitan (Wheat Meat) | Honey (Raw & Not Processed) | Garlic |
| Sprouted Wheat Bread (essene) | OILS | Ginger |
| Tapioca | Use all oils very sparingly | Mace |
| Wheat Bran | Almond | Marjoram |
| **LEGUMES** | Canola | Mint |
| Most legumes are good | Corn | Mustard Seeds |
| Adzuki Beans | Ghee | Neem Leaves |
| Black Beans | Sesame | Nutmeg |
| Black-eyed Peas | Sunflower | Orange Peel |
| Garbanzo Beans (ChickPeas) | | Oregano |
| Lentils (Red & Brown) | | Paprika |
| Lima Beans | | Parsley |
| Mung Beans/Dal | | Peppermint |
| Tur Dal | | Pippali |
| Navy Beans | | Poppy Seeds |
| Peas (Dried) | | Rosemary |
| Pinto Beans | | Saffron |
| Soy Sausages | | Sage |
| Split Peas | | Savory |
| Tempeh | | Spearmint |

| | | |
|---|---|---|
| Tofu (Hot) | | Star Anise |
| White Bean | | Tarragon |
| | | Thyme |
| | | Turmeric |
| | | Vanilla |
| | | Wintergreen |

# PITTA:

This list is not all inclusive. Only eat when you are hungry, eat your last meal at least 3 hours before going to bed, reduce sour, salty, pungent foods, focus more on sweet, bitter and astringent foods, use oils moderately, foods should be cooling, eat herbs and spices that are cooling, reduce alcohol, warm foods (except during cold weather)

| FRUITS | VEGETABLES | VEGETABLES, cont. |
|---|---|---|
| Generally most sweet fruits, avoid sour | In general sweet and bitter vegetables | Parsley |
| Apples (sweet) | Acorn squash | Parsnips |
| Applesauce | Artichoke | Peas |
| Apricots (sweet) | Asparagus | Peppers (green) |
| Avocado (use moderately) | Beets (cooked) | Peppers, sweet |
| Berries (sweet) | Bell pepper | Potatoes, sweet and white |
| Cherries (sweet) | Bitter melon | Prickly pear (leaves) |
| Coconut | Broccoli | Pumpkin |
| Dates | Brussels sprouts | Radishes (cooked) |
| Durian (in season in small amounts) | Burdock root | Rutabaga |
| Figs | Butternut squash | Spaghetti squash |
| Grapes (red and purple) | Cabbage | Sprouts (not spicy) |
| Guava (use moderately) | Carrots (cooked) | Squash, winter and summer |
| Longan (seasonal) | Cauliflower | Summer squash |
| Lychees (use moderately) | Celery | Scallopini Squash |
| Mangoes (ripe) | Cilantro/Coriander | Taro root |
| Melons | Corn (fresh) | Wheatgrass sprouts |
| Papaya (sweet) | Cucumber | Watercress |

| | | |
|---|---|---|
| Oranges (sweet, use moderately) | Dandelion greens | Winter squash |
| Pears | Fennel (anise) | Zucchini |
| Persimmon (use moderately) | Green beans | **BEVERAGES** |
| Pineapple (use moderately) | Jerusalem artichoke | Almond milk |
| Plums (sweet) | Kale | Aloe vera juice |
| Pomegranate (use moderately) | Leafy greens | Apple juice |
| Prunes | Leeks (cooked) | Apricot juice |
| Quince (sweet) | Lettuce | Berry juice (sweet) |
| Raisins | Mushrooms | Black tea |
| Rambutan (seasonal) | Okra | Carob |
| Watermelon | Olives, black | Cherry juice (sweet) |
| **GRAINS** | Onions (cooked and sweet) | Cool dairy drinks |
| Amaranth | **ANIMAL FOODS** | Grape juice |
| Barley | Chicken (white) | Mango juice |
| Cereal, dry | Eggs (albumen or white only) | Mixed vegetable juice |
| Couscous | Fish (freshwater) | Peach nectar |
| Crackers | Rabbit | Pear juice |
| Durham flour | Shrimp | Pomegranate juice |
| Granola | Turkey (white) | Prune juice |
| Oat bran | Venison | Rice milk |
| Oats (Cooked) | **CONDIMENTS** | Soy milk |
| Pancakes | Avoid or use very little salt | Vegetable bouillon |
| Pasta | Black Pepper* | **HERBAL TEAS** |
| Rice (basmati, white, wild) | Chutney, mango (sweet) | Alfalfa |
| Rice cakes | Coriander leaves | Bancha |

| | | |
|---|---|---|
| Sago | Sprouts | Barley |
| Seitan (wheat meat) | **NUTS** | Blackberry |
| Spelt | Almonds (soaked and peeled) | Borage |
| Sprouted wheat bread (essene) | Charole | Burdock |
| Tapioca | Coconut | Catnip |
| Wheat | **SEEDS** | Chamomile |
| Wheat bran | Flax | Chicory |
| **DAIRY** | Halva | Comfrey |
| Butter (unsalted) | Popcorn (no salt, buttered) | Dandelion |
| Cheese (soft, not aged, unsalted) | Psyllium | Fennel |
| Cottage cheese | Pumpkin | Ginger (fresh) |
| Cow's milk | Sunflower | Hibiscus |
| Goat's cheese (soft, unsalted) | **OILS** | Hops |
| Ice cream | For internal and external use | Jasmine |
| Yoghurt (freshly made and diluted) | Sunflower | Kukicha |
| **LEGUMES** | Ghee | Lavender |
| Avoid lentils | Canola | Lemon balm |
| Adzuki beans | Olive | Lemon grass |
| Black beans | Soy | Licorice |
| Black-eyed peas | Flaxseed | Marshmallow |
| Chickpeas (garbanzo beans) | Primrose | Nettle |
| Kidney beans | Walnut | Oat straw |
| Lima beans | External use only | Passion flower |
| Mung beans | Avocado | Peppermint |
| Mung dal | Coconut | Raspberry |

| | | |
|---|---|---|
| Navy beans | **SWEETENERS** | Red clover |
| Peas (dried) | Use honey (raw and young) only in moderation | Sarsaparilla |
| Pinto beans | Barley Malt Syrup | Spearmint |
| Soybeans | Brown Rice Syrup | Strawberry |
| Soy cheese | Maple Syrup | Violet |
| Soy milk | Fruit Juice Concentrates | Wintergreen |
| Split peas | Sugar Cane Juice | Yarrow |
| Tempeh | | |
| Tofu | | |
| White beans | | |
| **SPICES** | | |
| Cooling spices are good | | |
| Basil (fresh) | | |
| Cardamom | | |
| Cinnamon | | |
| Coriander | | |
| Cumin | | |
| Curry leaves | | |
| Dill | | |
| Fennel | | |
| Ginger (fresh and young) | | |
| Mint | | |
| Parsley | | |
| Peppermint | | |
| Saffron | | |
| Spearmint | | |
| Turmeric | | |
| Wintergreen | | |

# VATA:

This list is not all inclusive. Only eat when you are hungry, eat your last meal at least 3 hours before going to bed, Vata does well with 3 meals a day, reduce bitter, pungent, astringent foods, focus more on sweet, sour and salty foods, use oils liberally, foods should be warm, cooked, spicy, flavorful, heavy, grounding. Use herbs and spices, and reduce raw foods

| FRUITS | VEGETABLES | GRAINS and LEGUMES |
|---|---|---|
| Generally most sweet fruits | In general vegetables should be cooked | Legumes in moderation |
| Apples | Asparagus | Aduki Beans |
| Applesauce | Beets | Amaranth |
| Apricots | Cabbage (cooked) | Black Lentils |
| Avocados | Carrots | Durham flour |
| Bananas | Cauliflower | Lentils (red) |
| Berries | Cilantro/Coriander | Mung beans |
| Cherries | Cucumber | Mung dal |
| Coconut | Daikon radish | Oats |
| Dates (fresh) | Fennel (anise) | Oats (cooked) |
| Durian (seasonal) | Garlic | Pancakes |
| Figs (fresh) | Green beans | Quinoa |
| Grapefruit | Green chillies | Rice (all kinds) |
| Grapes | Jerusalem artichoke | Seitan (wheat meat) |
| Guava | Leafy greens | Soya cheese |
| Kiwifruit | Leeks | Soya milk |
| Lemons | Lettuce | Soya sausage |
| Limes | Mustard greens | Sprouted wheat bread |
| Longan (seasonal) | Okra | Tofu |
| Lychees | Olives (black) | Turdal |

| | | |
|---|---|---|
| Mangoes | Onions (cooked) | Urad dal |
| Melons (sweet) | Parsley | Wheat |
| Oranges | Parsnip | **BEVERAGES** |
| Papaya | Peas (cooked) | all fruit juices to be freshly made |
| Peaches | Potatoes (sweet) | Almond milk |
| Pineapple | Pumpkin | Aloe vera juice |
| Plums | Radishes (cooked) | Apricot juice |
| Prunes (cooked) | Rutabaga | Berry juice (except cranberry) |
| Raisins (soaked) | Spaghetti squash | Carob |
| Rambutan (seasonal) | Spinach (cooked) | Carrot juice |
| Rhubarb | Sprouts | Chai (hot spiced milk) |
| Strawberries | Squash summer and winter | Grain coffee |
| DAIRY | Taro root | Grape juice |
| Butter | Turnip greens | Grapefruit juice |
| Buttermilk | Watercress | Lemonade (freshly made) |
| Cheese (hard) | Zucchini | Mango juice |
| Cheese (soft) | **CONDIMENTS** | Miso broth |
| Cottage cheese | Black pepper | Orange juice |
| Cows milk | Chutney (mango) - sweet or spicy | Papaya juice |
| Ghee | Chili peppers | Peach nectar |
| Goats cheese | Coriander leaves | Pineapple juice |
| Goats milk | Dulse | Rice milk |
| Ice cream | Gomasio | Soya milk (hot and well spiced) |
| Sour cream | Hijiki | **HERB TEAS** |
| Yoghurt (diluted and spiced) | Kelp | Ajwan |

| | | |
|---|---|---|
| **ANIMAL FOOD** | Ketchup | Bancha |
| Chicken (dark) | Kombu | Catnip |
| Chicken (white)* | Lemon | Chamomile |
| Duck | Lime | Chicory |
| Eggs | Lime pickle | Chrysanthemum |
| Fish - freshwater or sea | Mango pickle | Clove |
| Lamb (as broth) | Mayonnaise | Comfrey |
| Salmon | Mustard | Elder flower |
| Sardines | Pickles | Eucalyptus |
| Seafood | Salt | Fennel |
| Shrimps | Scallions | Fenugreek |
| Tunafish | Seaweed | Ginger (fresh) |
| Turkey (dark) | Soy sauce | Hawthorn |
| **NUTS** | Sprouts | Juniper berry |
| In moderation | Tamari | Kukicha |
| Almonds | Vinegar | Lavender |
| Black walnuts | **SEEDS** | Lemongrass |
| Brazil nuts | Chia | Licorice |
| Cashews | Flax | Marshmallow |
| Charole | Halva | Oat straw |
| Coconut | Pumpkin | Orange peel |
| Filberts | Sesame | Penny royal |
| Hazelnuts | Sunflower | Peppermint |
| Macadamia nuts | Tahini | Raspberry |
| Peanuts | **OILS** | Rosehips |
| Pecans | Sesame | Saffron |
| Pine nuts | Ghee | Sage |
| Pistachios | Olive | Sarsaparilla |
| Walnuts | Coconut | Sassafras |
| **SPICES** | **SWEETENERS** | Spearmint |

| | | |
|---|---|---|
| Ajwan | Barley malt | Strawberry |
| Allspice | Fructose | Wintergreen |
| Almond extract | Fruit juice concentrates | **FOOD SUPPLEMENTS** |
| Anise | Honey - raw and not processed | Aloe vera juice |
| Basil | Molasses | Bee pollen |
| Bay leaf | Rice syrup | Amino acids |
| Black pepper | Sucanat | Minerals |
| Cardamom | Turbinado | Calcium |
| Cayenne | | Copper iron |
| Cinnamon | | Magnesium |
| Cloves | | Zinc |
| Coriander | | Royal jelly |
| Cumin | | Spirulina |
| Curry leaves | | Blue green algae |
| Dill | | Vitamins A and B complex |
| Fennel | | B12 - C - D and E |
| Fenugreek* | | |
| Garlic | | |
| Ginger | | |
| Mace | | |
| Marjoram | | |
| Mint | | |
| Mustard seed | | |
| Nutmeg | | |
| Orange peel | | |
| Oregano | | |
| Paprika | | |
| Parsley | | |
| Peppermint | | |
| Pippali | | |

| | | |
|---|---|---|
| Poppy seeds | | |
| Rosemary | | |
| Saffron | | |
| Salt | | |
| Savory | | |
| Spearmint | | |
| Star anise | | |
| Tarragon | | |
| Thyme | | |
| Turmeric | | |
| Vanilla | | |
| Wintergreen | | |

This picture was drawn by someone high on meth. It was drawn on a huge piece of poster paper. Hours were spent on the dots and the intricate detail. Each of the shaded areas is literally hundreds of dots; it's difficult to see at this size. As soon as the drawing was done, the person grabbed a lighter and attempted to burn it. It left the top edge charred. Someone pulled it out of the trash and kept it. Whoever drew it and whoever pulled it out of the trash both recognized the monster addiction had become in their life.

# TWELVE STEPS OF ALCOHOLICS ANONYMOUS

**Step One:** Admit that you are powerless over alcohol (your addiction), and that your life has become unmanageable.

**Step Two:** Come to believe that a power greater than yourself can restore your sanity.

**Step Three:** Make a decision to turn your will and your life over to the care of (your higher power) as you understand it (him).

**Step Four:** Make a searching and fearless moral inventory of yourself.

**Step Five:** Admit to (your higher power), to yourself, and to other human beings the exact nature of your wrongs.

**Step Six:** Be entirely ready to have (your higher power) remove all of these defects of character.

**Step Seven:** Humbly ask (your higher power) to remove all of your shortcomings.

**Step Eight:** Make a list of all persons I have harmed and become willing to make amends to them all.

**Step Nine:** Make direct amends to such people, wherever possible, except when to do so would injure them or others.

**Step Ten:** Continue to take personal inventory and when you are wrong, promptly admit it.

**Step Eleven:** Seek through prayer and meditation to improve your conscious contact with (your higher power), as you understand (him) (it), praying only for knowledge of its will for you and the power to carry that out.

**Step Twelve:** Having had a spiritual awakening as the result of these steps, try to carry this message to (addicts), and to practice these principles in all affairs.

# TWELVE TRADITIONS OF ALCOHOLICS ANONYMOUS

**Tradition One:** Common welfare should come first; personal recovery depends on AA unity.

**Tradition Two:** For this group purpose there is but one ultimate authority - a loving, higher power as it may express itself in this group conscience. The leaders are but trusted servants, they do not govern.

**Tradition Three:** The only requirement for A.A. membership is a desire to stop drinking (using).

**Tradition Four:** Each group should be autonomous except in matters affecting other groups or A.A. as a whole.

**Tradition Five:** Each group has but one primary purpose - to carry its message to the alcoholic (addict) who still suffers.

**Tradition Six:** An A.A. group ought never endorse, finance, or lend the A.A. name to any related facility our outside enterprise, lest problems of money, property, and prestige divert us from our primary purpose.

**Tradition Seven:** Every A.A. group ought to be fully self-supporting, declining outside contributions.

**Tradition Eight:** Alcoholics Anonymous should remain forever nonprofessional, but service centers may employ special workers.

**Tradition Nine:** A.A. as such, ought never be organized; but may create service boards or committees directly responsible for those they serve.

**Tradition Ten:** Alcoholics Anonymous has no opinion on outside issues; hence the A.A. name ought never be drawn into public controversy.

**Tradition Eleven:** Public Relations policy is based on attraction rather than promotion; we need always maintain personal anonymity at the level of press, radio and films.

**Tradition Twelve:** Anonymity is the spiritual foundation of all traditions, ever reminding us to place principles before personalities.

# REFERENCES

Edenberg, Dr.Howard J., https://pubs.niaaa.nih.gov/
publications/arh301/3-4.htm
https://www.psychologytoday.com/us/basics/highly-sensitive-
person#:~:text=Overall%2C%20about%2015%20to%20
20,things%20are%20likely%20to%20occur.
https://nida.nih.gov/publications/drugfacts/
understanding-drug-use-addiction

Maydych, Viktoriya, 2019
https://www.ncbi.nlm.nih.gov/pmc/articles/
PMC6491771/#:~:text=Chronic%20exposure%20to%20
stressors%20causes,symptoms%20(Rohleder%2C%202014).

The Great Debate: Nature vs. Nurture; Genetics and Abuse, 2022
https://americanaddictioncenters.org/
adult-addiction-treatment-programs/nature-vs-nurture

Rao, T.S. Sathyanarayana, The Biochemistry of Belief, 2009
https://www.ncbi.nlm.nih.gov/pmc/articles/PMC2802367/
https://newsinhealth.nih.gov/2021/06/mindfulness-your-health
https://science.nasa.gov/astrophysics/focus-areas/what-is-dark-energy

Wehr, Thomas A., 2018, Bipolar Mood Cycles Associated with Lunar Entrainment of a Circadian Rhythm
https://www.ncbi.nlm.nih.gov/pmc/articles/PMC6089884/
https://news.stanford.edu/2018/06/11/
four-ways-human-mind-shapes-reality/

Chevalier, Gaetan, 2012; 2012: 291541. Published online 2012 Jan 12. doi: 10.1155/2012/291541
https://www.ncbi.nlm.nih.gov/pmc/articles/PMC3265077/
J Environ Public Health.

Alda, Marta, 2016; 7: 651–659. Published online 2016 Feb 22. doi: 10.1007/s12671-016-0500-5
https://www.ncbi.nlm.nih.gov/pmc/articles/PMC4859856/
Mindfulness (N Y).

Oschman, James L., 2015, The Effects of Grounding (Earthing)
https://pubmed.ncbi.nlm.nih.gov/25848315/

Privitera, Adam John, 2023, Sensation and Perception
https://nobaproject.com/modules/sensation-and-perception

Tiller, William A., Clinical Trial: J Altern Complement Med: 2012 Apr;18(4):379-81. doi: 10.1089/acm.2011.0817
https://pbmed.ncbi.nlm.nih.gov/22515797/

Yale School of Medicine: Yale Medicine Magazine, 2012
https://medicine.yale.edu/news/yale-medicine-magazine/article/
new-study-finds-links-between-meditation-and-brain/

Augusto Del Melo Reis, Ricardo, 2021, Quality of Life and a
Surveillant Endocannabinoid System
https://www.ncbi.nlm.nih.gov/pmc/articles/PMC8581450/

# ABOUT THE AUTHOR

This is the story of a mother and her son. The addiction of her youngest son provided some of the most painful, yet encouraging lessons she never thought she'd learn. The process of coping with the conflicting emotions created by watching her child suffer, with those leading her toward her own life path, provided the tools and the courage to share the truthful, yet sometimes painful realities of loving an addict. She is the mother of 4, and grandmother of 6. The road to healing can be long and difficult, but there is nothing that cannot be overcome. There is a lesson in all suffering, crisis, and conflict, if only we pay attention. By sharing this story, she risks the relationship of friends, family and acquaintances, but her hope is that by sharing the knowledge that she has gained, you might be assisted in your journey. Her hope is that you are able to find even one piece of advice within the pages of this book that may help lead you to a path of new happiness. Life is never perfect, and we shouldn't expect it to be. However, when such incredible suffering is in our midst, we can still make the choice to be happy moment by moment.